The Internet Politician's Lessons In Management

Anthony R. Haslage

The Internet Politician's Lessons In Management

Anthony R. Haslage

First Edition

Disclaimer

]===>
Cover Design: Anthony R. Haslage

Art Direction: Anthony R. Haslage

For educational, press and sales permission requests, please contact the publisher at:

http://Tony.Haslage.Net/

Library of Congress Cataloging-in-Publication number: …

IBSN: 9798866945917

BISAC category code: …

<===[

Contents

© Haslage Net Enterprises

]==>

<==[

```
]=============================================>
```



```
<=============================================[
```

Preface

The goal of this document is to provide an updated version of the author's original Master's Thesis (2010-2012). Most of this content could be found in the previously published, "The 21st Century Workplace: A HR & EEO Guide". What remains in this document consists of some updated information, the removal of some outdated information and some new information. Plus, a little bit of better organization of its contents.

None of the images within this document were created by artificial intelligence.

]===>

About the Author

Anthony Haslage was born in Lorain, Ohio, where he has lived for most of his life. After completing grade school, Haslage worked intermittently up until September 2001. After a year of inactivity, he decided to attend college at Lorain County Community College in Elyria, Ohio where he later earned associate degrees in both applied business and the arts. Haslage then attended Kent State University where he earned a Bachelor of Business Administration and later attended the University of Akron where he earned a Master of Public Administration.

From the age of 10, Haslage was engaged in community service. Initially, as a member of the Boy Scouts of America, Haslage was involved in a number of clean-up and repainting efforts. Once leaving his troop, Haslage became further involved in his community by

<===[

]===>

offering his services to local businesses and organizations. This eventually led to Haslage getting involved in local politics.

During his time in college and a decade afterwards, Haslage remained involved in whatever community he was a part. While in college, Haslage spent four years writing for the college newspaper and two years serving on the student senate, in addition to being an officer in a number of student organizations. When he was not involved in college activities, Haslage served as an officer for a number of non-profit organizations. He was responsible for the creation and operation of a number of fundraising efforts. After completing college, Haslage was hired to positions within the video game industry, among others.

<===[

Abstract

Over the years, the author has been encouraged to write a management handbook for young businesses and organizations. As a fan of working smarter and not harder, it would be smarter to create a general document for all young businesses and organizations to utilize. No one expects any business or organization to follow this document as written through their entire life, but rather consider it a living document that would be updated and built-upon as time progresses.

Henceforth, while the term "organization" will be used throughout this document, it is not singling out non-profit organizations from for-profit businesses. The term is being used generally to encompass all corporation types.

]==>

Welcome

As a new member of the team, you are expected to retain a professional appearance and attitude within the confines of your work agreement, no matter how formal or informal it may have been. While there may be times where we may be lackadaisical in the enforcement of workplace policies in an effort to improve overall morale, there are some occasions and situations where we cannot ignore violations of our policies. The one thing that we must not do is set a negative precedence in those situations.

The government has created a number of guidelines and laws for how businesses must handle certain situations and if we were to ignore certain issues, all of us could lose our jobs. Thus, follow our policies

<===[

]===>

and report any issues to your direct supervisor or their

supervisor, if they are unavailable.

<====================================[

Mitigation & Response

> ## "AN OUNCE OF PREVENTION IS WORTH A POUND OF CURE."
> ## – BENJAMIN FRANKLIN

It has been said more than once, but organizations need to have plans in place to prevent issues and if that fails, resolve issues. No one can see every possible outcome of every possible situation that may arise. Mitigation is simply a means of being proactive in hopes of preventing issues from arising that everyone would agree should not arise. The response after an issue arises requires one to be reactive. Being reactive almost

]===>
always costs more than being proactive. We have always subscribed to the adage of "plan for the worst and hope for the best".

What is included in all of this research and personal observation is a bit of logic. It does not take a Warren Buffett level of experience and intelligence to figure out if "A" happens and "B" may be why. Another good adage keep in mind is that "the simplest answer is normally the best". The facts and numbers do not lie and as time goes on, the consequences for an organization not performing its due diligence only serves to cost it more money.

Does everything in this document cover all of the possible outcomes? We wish, but it does cover the broad strokes. Remember, Benjamin Franklin once said that, "An ounce of prevention is worth a pound of cure."

<===[

]===>

Equal Employment Opportunity

Our organization does not discriminate by age, color, disability, gender, gender identity, national origin, race, religion, sexual orientation or any other category under the law. Applicants are selected purely based upon a combination their ability, aptitude, education, experience and if required, the successful completion of background checks and testing.

<===[

]===>

Hiring & Firing

There are a lot of considerations that must be made when it comes to hiring. The first task is finding out if the open position has any type of job description. A job description usually includes such things as the position's full title, duties, responsibilities and any specifications that the applicants will need to know in advance of applying. A thorough job analysis can normally root out this information. (Dessler, pp. 251-2)

One must also consider the line of questions that is needed to thoroughly conduct the interviews. It is best that the planned interview questions are both uniform and open-ended for all candidates. However, if an opening arises in the process to explore the responses of any individual candidates, doing so will provide insight into how the candidate functions or thinks. Just keep in mind not to pry too deeply as at some point the

<==[

]===>
discussion will trail away from information needed for

the position to being too much information.   The last

thing an organization needs is a former candidate

threatening a lawsuit because they felt discriminated

against because of information they had disclosed in the

interview. (Dessler, p. 268)

The Human Resources and the Equal Employment

Opportunity departments, assuming that they are not

the same, need to work together to ensure that fair

hiring practices is being considered.   Hiring individuals

based on merit is the best approach.   However, some

states have laws that enforce quotas on minority

recruitment.   In addition, some candidates may fall

under the American Disabilities Act and if the

organization is not prepared to support candidates with

special needs, they must be willing to adapt.   Those that

<===[

]===>

are not willing to adapt and avoid making hires based on that fact will be open to legal action against any candidates that believe that they may have been wronged.

The location of where interviews are conducted can occur in any number of ways. In this age of technology, some candidates do not necessarily live local to the organization's headquarters and since travel costs are steadily on the rise, using a means of interviewing via the Internet is preferred. While most organizations still prefer in-person meetings, Internet-based interviews are convenient, inexpensive and allow candidates to feel more relaxed during the interview process. For those that do prefer in-person meetings, they need to be conducted in a visible location. The old method of interviewing individuals in walled-off offices with no

<==[

]==>

witnesses can open the door to unethical individuals taking advantage and creating a means for legal wrangling. It is often recommended that in-person interviews be conducted in open conference rooms or cubical spaces. It would also be recommended that two staff members participate in the interview process, locally or remotely.

Be it the first or third interview of the same candidate, a rapport needs to be established. A few questions about hot topics in the news or local happenings are good for starters, just remember avoid hot button issues such as politics, religion or sports. Once the interview officially begins, double-check to ensure that the application information submitted is correct and to weed out any inconsistencies. When it comes time to ask the important questions, do not be

<====================================[

]===>

afraid to ask for elaboration, if needed. Remember to write notes pertaining to responses, be they verbal or non-verbal. (Dessler, p. 268)

If by the end of the interview there is an idea either way on the possibility of hiring the individual, let them know. If the decision will take longer, remember to issue a statement to the candidate in one form or another once a decision is made. If the candidate was pleasant and could possibly fill another position, encourage them to apply or recommend them for the position. Otherwise, take the opportunity to promote the organization and thank them for their time. Once the interview has concluded, reflect and make additional notes, as needed. (Dessler, p. 268)

At some point in the hiring process, the opportunity to check references may arise. When

<===[

]==>
checking education or job references, many

organizations will only provide information pertaining to

the person's job title, a job description summary and

how long they were employed. Sometimes this limit in

information is policy, other times it depends on the

disposition of the person responding. By checking the

education and job references, you are both confirming

the legitimacy of the information provided and

attempting to gather information on the candidate's

experience. When checking personal or professional

references, you seek to get the opinions of colleagues

and friends about a candidate as a person. It is safe to

assume that these individuals may be exaggerating the

positives and downplaying the negatives. Do not apply

the same amount of weight to personal references that

]===>
you do professional ones and allow job references the

most weight.

Once all of the relevant data is gathered on each of

the candidates, use a fair process to select the best

candidate for the position. The preferred and possibly

easiest method is a double-blind evaluation. Two

individuals, uninvolved in the hiring process, weed

through the mass of data without names or any

demographic information and select candidates purely

based on merit, ranking each accordingly. This ensures

that no one can argue that the process was somehow

tainted. If and when a candidate is selected, inform

them and allow time to respond to accept. If they

accept, inform the other candidates that they were not

selected. If they do not accept, contact the next ranked

<===[

]===>

candidate. Either way, do not inform anyone that they were not selected until someone accepts the position.

On the plus side, firing an employee is a lot easier than hiring one, in most cases. Sure, there are those cases where someone loses a job due to reasons that have nothing to do with them, but that is not something that is being covered here as those reasons are typically straight-forward. If an individual does something wrong, as long as there is proof and a clear rule against the action, they can be fired at minimal detriment to the organization. Many of the states in the United States fall under Employment-at-Will. This means that employees have the right to apply, quit, strike or simply stop working and employers have the right to hire, fire or lay-off employees for any or no reason. However, organizations that fire without a good reason may be

<====================================[

]===>
forced   to   pay   unemployment   insurance   or   find

themselves in court.

]===>

The Fair Pay Act

In 2012, a few surveys were conducted in the United States to evaluate the percentages women and minorities were paid in comparison to white males holding a similar position with similar duties. On average, minority males earned approximately 90 percent of their white counterparts. On the other hand, white women earned an average of approximately 70 percent, while minority women earned as much as 63 percent of their white male counterparts.

While a glass ceiling is an upper limitation of position based on a specific gender or race, discrepancies in pay are more aimed at a person's worth as a human being. Compared to white males in similar positions with similar duties, there is no statistical data that proves that women or minorities perform at any less of a level.

<====================================[

]==>

To pay anyone less in a role simply based upon their sex or race has been a practice in play since the beginning of capitalism. Sexism and racism play a significant role in pay discrepancies. Women are seen as emotional and weak while minorities are seen as mentally inferior. These factors are then considered and deducted from pay as a means of covering perceived risk.

In 2009, the Lilly Ledbetter Fair Pay Act amended "Title VII of the Civil Rights Act of 1964 and the Age Discrimination in Employment Act of 1967" and modified "the operation of the Americans with Disabilities Act of 1990 and the Rehabilitation Act of 1973, to clarify that a discriminatory compensation decision or other practice that is unlawful under such Acts occurs each time compensation is paid pursuant to the discriminatory

<==[

]===>
compensation decision or other practice, and for other

purposes." (Lilly, 2009)

In essence, the Fair Pay Act states that if a person

is placed in a position and can perform the duties to its

specification, they should earn the full pay that is

entitled to them. This means that no decisions based on

gender, race, disability or age should be made in

consideration of pay. The Act also discloses that

violators will suffer an accrued liability for up to two

years and be forced to compensate affected parties.

Someone somewhere may be wondering if there is

a work around for this Act. Yes, there is and most

organizations do this naturally by creating tiers in

positions according to duties. The government and

major corporations do it and they typically list positions

<===[

]==>

by grades. At any rate, organizations limit their pool of talent by stacking positions too broadly.

If your organization builds parks and one job is lifting 250 and 100 pound bags all day, break it into two tiers. The first tier (Lifter I) is lifting 250 pound bags all day and the second tier (Lifter II) is lifting 100 pound bags all day. Those who cannot lift 250 pound bags will apply to the 100 pound bag job and vice versa. Of course the 250 pound bag job pays more because the weight is more and they take just as many trips as the 100 pound bag job does. If someone applies to lift the 250 pound bags and is unable to perform the duties, demote them to the 100 pound bag job. If they still cannot perform the duties of the 100 pound bag jobs, remove them. The entire point is that within each tier, there cannot be any form of discrimination.

<===[

]===>
The Glass Ceiling

There is a combination of factors as to why there may no longer be a glass ceiling. The most significant reason is Carly Fiorina becoming the chief executive officer of Hewlett-Packard in July 1999. However, while in general a glass ceiling may no longer exists, in some vocations they find having a glass ceiling necessary, though probably still for sexist reasons.

For those unfamiliar with the topic, Dictionary.Com defines the glass ceiling as "an upper limit to professional advancement, especially as imposed upon women that is not readily perceived or openly acknowledged." What it boils down to is that up to a specific point in time, women never found themselves as being part of the "Boy's Club." It was not until the 1990s that women found themselves in positions such as president or chief executive officer in any large

<===[

]===>
organizations, short of those notoriously serving strictly women.   Many statistics, sadly including sexual harassment complaints by men against women in power, back this assumption.

Consider the fact is that there are a few cases of glass ceilings for men as well. Until a recent point in history, rarely could men be found as nurses, working in flower shops or holding any other jobs where the general population believed that only women should occupy them. This is despite the fact that historically men may have held those positions. The glass ceiling concept is a two-way street. However, as times have changed, it has now begun to be less about gender and more about sexual preferences.

<===[

]===>
Group Interviewing

Group interviewing always seems like a good idea at the time and sometimes it is for the sake of convenience that it is even attempted. The reason anyone chooses to conduct a group interview is because they believe that having to ask a question only once amongst a group of people will ultimately save them some time. The decision to conduct a group interview is essentially a tradeoff between the quantity of time and the quality of interviewee responses. Frankly, it may save the tiniest bit of time, but only at the expense of receiving as much relevant information as possible. In the end, employers will have to pay even closer attention as they tread through every application and resume sorting out the relevant information that they seek, checking everything for factuality.

<==[

]==>

Surely, no one would conduct a group interview for multiple different positions at the same time. Such an endeavor would be difficult to keep track of and would ultimately not be best served in a group setting. Thus, it makes sense to interviewees that group interviews are a competition. To them, everyone is vying for the same job and the one with the best answers will win. As a result, group interviewing creates three different types of interviewees.

The first type of interviewee is the one with nothing to lose. If permitted to answer any questions after someone else, they will attempt to one-up the previous interviewee's answers. There is a significant chance that this interviewee is stretching the truth, if not simply making things up. It is very unlikely that this person will reach the next level of the hiring process if

<===[

]===>
not counteracted. To counteract this type of interviewee,
have them answer every question first. This will prevent
them from attempting to trump the answers of the other
interviewees and bring out a little bit more of the truth.

The second type of interviewee is the one with the
education and experience. They know that most
employers will sort through the hype to find the truth, so
they state only facts. These people will typically make it
to the next level of the hiring process.

The third type of interviewee is the one with little
or no education or experience. They are fairly new to
seeking employment and may lack the relevant
experience and knowledge that certain employers seek.
During the interview, they will most likely be very
reserved as they are unsure how to answer any of the
questions. Most of their responses will be very

<===[

]==>

minimalistic. If counteracted, as long as they can keep to the facts and answer the questions completely, they may see the next level in the hiring process. To counteract this type of interviewee, have them answer every question last. This will provide them with examples on how to correctly answer the questions being asked.

]===>
Background Checks

Getting a background check on a potential employee is a simple process and there are pre-employment information services that can make it even easier. As a means to save cost, potential employees can be asked to perform their own background checks via the local police department. This is done by providing the employee a sealed envelope.

Inside the envelope is a document for a police officer to read and complete. With the document is a new envelope that the police officer needs to fill, seal and mark before handing the completed and sealed document to the potential employee to be returned to the office. This process is not just inexpensive, but if the envelope is returned with no signs of tampering, then you can have a little assurance that perhaps this

<====================================[

]==>

potential employee may be honest. Otherwise, you can always engage potential employees with honesty testing.

However, there are a few considerations for this method of saving time and costs. First, is that the envelopes must be the security type with the tape. Lick and seal envelopes are too easy to steam open and close. Second, the police officer needs to mark the sealed portion of the envelope across the seam with some type of stamp. Once an envelope is opened, it is difficult to close it again with the stamp perfectly intact. And finally, always request the use of colored ink. Black ink can be a sign of a copied or modified document. You want the original.

These tips are aimed squarely at organizations with tight budgets. Executed effectively, the costs will

<==[

]==>

be minimal and the return will be greater through the efforts of honest potential employees.

During the course of the background check, and once a criminal record is determined as a potential means for elimination one way or another, one's finances may be of consideration. Often times, credit reports do not fully explain low credit ratings. Many organizations take low credit ratings to mean that a person is irresponsible with money and would be a financial risk to the organization. The fact is that sentiments such as those are purely discriminatory in nature. Sure, this type of discrimination may not be illegal, but a lot needs to be known before eliminating someone as a possible employee.

For those who attended public colleges and universities, the government does a lot to reduce the

<==[

]==>

costs for education. In Ohio, the costs of associate level degrees could be paid in it's entirely by the government. If not for the state government's initial assistance, many would have never considered attending any universities for additional degrees. After finishing university and depending upon the degree, students could accrue over 100,000 dollars in educational debt. They do not plan it, but the costs add up.

Here belies the problem. Just like most other people out there, we do not like owing anyone money. The fact that we owe anyone anything gives us more of a reason to work harder and pay our debts. This is a quality employers should embrace. Most of us work harder and tolerate a lot more when we are being relied upon by others, especially when money is involved.

<==[

]===>

The next time you run a credit check on a potential employee with a recent graduation date, consider the opportunity that you have in front of you before looking elsewhere.

<===[

]==>
Drug Testing

If it is good enough for the government, then it is good enough for your business. The problem is that until recently, drug testing was very expensive. Now with the take home cleansing kits that can be bought at the store, people have found ways to circumvent most drug testing. Drug testing on any schedule now gives potential employees a chance to cheat the system. To circumvent the cheat, drug testing needs to be almost impromptu. However, there are a few limits when performing impromptu drug testing.

A specific employee cannot be targeted for a drug test unless there is either a substantial amount of proof of drug use or a government entity requires that testing be conducted. To single out an employee for drug testing can be seen as harassment and may potentially become a legal issue. It is best to drug test an entire

<===[

]==>

work group and ensuring that individuals are not tested

together as a means to reduce the chances of cheating.

Drug testing counter-measures take an upwards of

four hours to be most effective. What they do is cleanse

one's system of chemicals released into the body by

various types of drugs including marijuana and hard

narcotics such as methamphetamines. To counteract the

counter, employers need to call potential employees

within an hour deadline to appear for drug testing. It

may seem cruel to provide such short notice, but most

organizations do not have the funds to play games. If

potential employees cannot make the deadline, then

they obviously were not prepared for the demand of the

position in which they had applied.

All of the effort to drug test means less if the

potential employee is not aware that you perform drug

<==[

]===>

testing. The simple mention that random drug testing is conducted will eliminate a lot of potential costs on its own by weeding out those who do not wish to forego drug use for employment. Why waste a test on someone who will fail? Plus, when do you call those who stick around to be drug tested, they cannot claim ignorance of not knowing that drug testing was going to be performed.

If a pre-employment drug testing center is not available in-house, a full service pre-employment drug testing center can normally be found in most cities. If all else fails, find a physician willing to offer their services at a bulk or contracted rate.

]===>
Reasonable Accommodations

The author used to volunteer for an organization that held their largest event during the worst part of winter. When we say largest, they mean in size, scale, scope, attendance, activities, food and so much more. A few years prior, the event had even incorporated a Support Services department for the physically disabled to assist its growing handicapped population.

In 2011, a blizzard the day before the event did not even hurt its attendance. In fact, the attendance numbers had been steadily increasing over the years. Their guest speakers were the tops in their industry and the organization flew them in from all over the country, even providing them with hotel rooms and meals in addition to their contracted pay. The around-the-clock entertainment opportunities available to the attendees

<===[

]==>

were vast and the many ways to spend one's money was mind-boggling.

However, what many of the volunteers did not know was that the organization was in trouble and that suddenly, its ownership had changed hands. Apparently, a former senior manager embezzled heavily, forcing the previous owners to sell the organization to make up their losses. The new owner, learning from the mistakes of the previous owner, decided to retain a lawyer to protect his investment. The problem was that the owner began to rely too heavily on the lawyer to respond to even the simplest of concerns. To top it off, the lawyer kept the typical nine to five business hours and did not work weekends. This was a critical issue for an event where half of it occurred over the course of a weekend and ran 24-hours a day.

<==[

]===>
It was Saturday evening and it was the busiest day of the entire event. As with every activity at the event, there was a space created so that physically disabled attendees could safely participate. Those that suffered any physical disability would receive a special sticker on their badge that indicated that they would require assistance finding their seats. For those in wheelchairs, seats were removed from rows so they could park without being blocked or blocking others. For those with vision problems, they were given seating within the first few rows. For those with hearing problems, depending on the event type, an American Sign Language (ASL) interpreter was on hand, closed-captioning was used or a special bass speaker was provided so they could feel any sound.

<===[

]===>

The most popular activity of Saturday evening was a dance. Some of the volunteers could only assist during the weekend. So, when the staff leaders assigned many of the people, those people had not been tested in other scenarios to evaluate strengths and weaknesses. One of the staff leaders had assigned a young gentleman volunteer to be the dance's bouncer. His job was simple, allow people to enter until the activity was full and to assist those with physical disabilities to the space set aside for them.

Within a half hour after the dance began, three complaints had been reported to the Support Services department stating that the bouncer was not permitting anyone with a handicap into the dance. After another half hour had passed, the complaints were up to seven. The Support Services department director was contacted

<==[

]===>

to investigate and reported back that he saw no reason for anyone to have been denied as the spaces set aside for handicapped individuals were empty. The Support Services department director then contacted his supervisor and she investigated. After another half hour, she reported that the issue was that the young gentleman volunteer who was assigned to be the bouncer was unable to read the badges due to having poor vision. He was simply identifying the badges based by their shape and general color scheme because he was unable to read any of the print on the badges, including the stickers for the physically disabled. Because of this volunteer's disability, the supervisor feared removing the volunteer from his position in fear that somehow the event could be sued for discrimination based on his disability. Eventually the news got to the owner who

<===[

]===>
then called his lawyer over and over again until the lawyer picked up the telephone so he could ask if the volunteer could be removed from his position without fear of legal reprisal. The lawyer, upset that he was bothered while he slept, cited an abridged form of the Americans with Disabilities Act.

The Americans with Disabilities Act (ADA) was established in 1990, as a means to discourage discrimination against individuals with disabilities in the workplace as well as provide reasonable accommodations to overcome most disabilities. It also includes protections against discriminatory actions during hiring and firing processes, but the focus of this topic is based squarely on someone already in a position. (EEOC, 2002)

<===[

]==>
    The Americans with Disabilities Act does not

typically cover volunteers, unless they are getting some

form of compensation. (JAN, 2012) In the case of this

event, many volunteers were compensated with a hotel

room and free meals, so this may have also been the

case with the young gentleman volunteer.   Assuming

that   the   aforementioned   is   true,   reasonable

accommodations could have been made in many ways

for this volunteer.   The easiest route would have been

providing a magnifying glass to the volunteer. Another

option would be assigning an additional volunteer who

would simply assist the handicapped.   Otherwise, the

volunteer could have been assigned to a vacant position.

(ADA, 2009)

    By the time the event owner had spoken with his

lawyer and reported the results of his conversation to

<===[

]==>
the supervisor, it was already after midnight. By that
time, most of the people who were denied access to the
dance had filed their complaints and found something
else to do.

Short of dismissing the volunteer based upon his
disability, the supervisor and owner did not have to
escalate the issue to the point of seeking legal counsel.
There were other duties that the volunteer could have
been assigned to work. Even considering the recent
issues within management, there was a slight bit of
overreaction to the fear of being sued. The law does not
exist to punish honest people. Frankly, a lot of the laws
that we have exist because as much as we would like to
think otherwise, common sense is not very common. To
wrap it up, the volunteer asked to help. Chances are

<==[

]==>
that if he would have been asked, he would have most

likely been glad to take up another assignment.

<===[

]===>
Politics: Benefits, Pay & Unions

The United States government has a lot to say about how we run our organizations and they do it by making them laws. The law says that we must pay at least some specific amount of money for hourly work, even less if tips are involved. The law also says that if we hire people under the age of 18, they may only work so long during the week and between certain hours. More recent laws even say that organizations that earn a certain amount of revenue each year must also provide a certain level of benefits to each employee. It all boils down to a combination of political forces deciding that our national interests are best served if our workforce is well-paid and healthy. Most of us can agree on that fact. However some of us can also agree that maybe the approaches chosen are not the best options.

<===[

]===>

Historically, through collective bargaining unions have served as a great model for estimating the ideal level of benefits and pay employees should receive. Unions have also been credited for inspiring the workplace laws that we now have. Before unions, employees were made to suffer in deplorable working conditions, for little benefits or pay.

As the years have passed, the importance of unions has wavered because the government is taking a more active role in regulating how a workplace must function. In more recent years, unions have found themselves relegated into a few niches. Unions are most likely found in locations where there is a large, unskilled workforce as well as where personal safety may be a concern, such as in the automotive, construction and

<===[

]===>
medical industries. The government also utilizes unions, such as for aviation and education.

Just like everything else in this world, there are down and up sides. Some types of unions are difficult to disband even if a majority of employees decide they no longer wish to be part. Depending upon the specific union, it can also sometimes be difficult to terminate a bad employee. Let us not forget the argument of management versus labor. For some, having a union succinctly ends the family-like atmosphere in exchange for a more corporate one. However, it is simply a lot easier to collectively bargain than it is to do it on the individual level for hundreds, if not thousands, of employees. Unions have also been known to save both time and money for the employer. Depending upon the specific union, if they are capable of working more

<==[

]===>

closely with the employer, they can even take over many of the human resource management functions.

On the employees' end, no matter who regulates their pay and benefits, it has to be at least the minimum established by law. Those that have chosen to be a member of a union should be paid at least the same as they had been paid prior to the union and after union fees. Those choosing to be either a member of a union or not should not suffer a penalty. Of course, if employees decide not to partake in the union, the employer's direct pay and benefit package may not necessarily be as good as what being part of the union may offer. Since time is money, some employers may see employees that do not join the union as an opportunity to save even more cash. Part of how a union saves money is because the larger the group is,

<==[

]==>

the less expensive the benefits packages typically are per union member.

Thanks to what the unions have started, many employers treat their employees very well. In fact, some employers fear unionization so much that they offer benefit and pay packages far superior to what some unions could ever offer.

Processes: Informal & Formal

Particularly in processes handling disciplinary action, there needs to be a means to escalate the level of action and response. The level of action and response is made more severe as the processes switch from verbal to written and informal to formal.

The first level is the lowest form of informal action and is usually a simple verbal communication. Verbal warnings are not generally recorded and are generally considered as a consideration for one's rare questionable actions.

The second level is still informal, but this time sent via electronic communications as a reminder of a previous warning. Again, recording the response is not necessary beyond the record in the sent box of the e-mail.

]==>

The third level is the beginning of a formal process. It is most commonly associated with the cease and desist letter. At this point it is recommended that all actions end else the next level will not be pleasant. It is also at this point that documentation be made in personnel files and via other sources that need to be informed of the action and response.

Finally, the end of the formal process is usually the last step leading to termination or legal action. Some call these processes the "three strikes and you are out" rule. The purpose is to give everyone a "fair shake," but not seeming too lenient towards offenders who do not seem to understand they are being told to stop whatever actions they have been taking.

There is one caveat. If the decision is not made to make record of all informal process, some people may

<==[

]=======================================>
abuse the system.   It is wise to share with other

administrators when informal action is taken.

<=====================================[

]===>
Team Meetings

Prior to the start of every shift, there should be a short meeting to discuss the plans of the day with the employees and review any concerns from the previous shift. This is the best opportunity to ensure that all employees are accounted for and that everyone is on the same page. There is nothing worse than an employee not knowing what they should be doing, instead doing what they think they should be doing and working against the common goal.

A few large chain stores seem to think that shift meetings are the appropriate time to gather everyone to cheer and pray. Someone at some point told them that doing so would create a unified work force that feels more like a family. The problem is that many people have no desire to be in another family and find prayer in the workplace insulting. Obviously, cheers and prayers

<===[

]==>

at a family-orientated, religious or spiritual organization

is an exception to the rule.

Individuals forced into or removed from cheering

or praying in the workplace feel like outsiders. Not

everyone has an outgoing personality, nor is everyone

religious or even spiritual. Organizations that skip the

cheers and prayers are no better off without them.

What happens is the allocation of output by those

involved goes up for a short time and those who are not

involved have less of an output for a short time. Better

results are gained by simply allowing employees an

opportunity to speak up at the shift meetings so that

whatever weighs heavily on them is heard. Plus, it is

comforting to employees when they feel they have been

heard and as a result, output increases.

<==[

Workplace Conduct

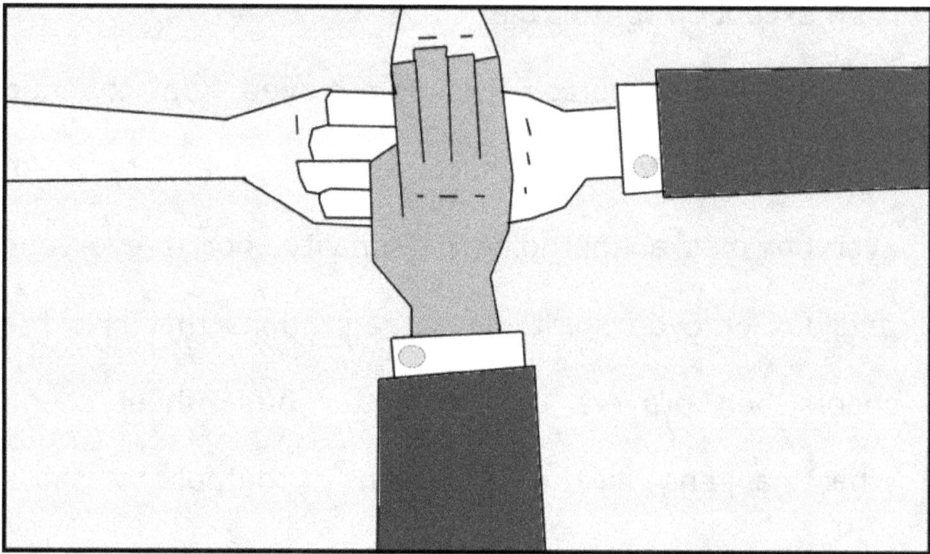

To eliminate any confusion and no matter the clientele, we shall refer to all those that our organization serves as customers. Since we may provide any number of products or services, even if they cost something or nothing, we should still strive for a positive experience for all involved.

]==>
Customer Service

While you are amongst customers, you must have at least a neutral, if not a positive attitude. One of our objectives is to provide a pleasant experience to those that we are here to serve and a negative attitude only serves to make our objective harder to reach.

Always use family-friendly language while around customers. It is recommended that we practice the use of family-family language even when not around those that we serve as not doing so can be construed as harassment by fellow co-workers. It is also recommended that conversations involving the following topics be avoided:

- Politics

- Religion

- Sports

<====================================[

Sell Yourself, Sell the Organization

If you can present yourself in a professional and positive manner while you serve a customer, you will not only be liked by the customer, they will like the organization.   It may not work every time, but it certainly does work most of the time.   Here are some useful tips:

- Smile
- Greet new customers as they enter the organization.
- Speak professionally
- Strike up a conversation.
    - Using humor can be risky, especially if the customer is unfamiliar with the topic of discussion.
- ALWAYS listen attentively.

]==>

- Treat the customers like they are important to us, because they are!

- DO NOT chew gum, eat or use mobile devices while in view of customers.

- NEVER re-greet customers that have been greeted by other employees. It is an instant turn-off for some customers as they may see it as hostile and intrusive hard sales tactic.

  - Most customers respond well to soft sales tactics.

    - Hard sales tactics are a hands-on approach to sales where the salesperson hovers around the customer, frequently checking up on them and recommending items to purchase.

<==[

]===>

- Soft sales tactics are a hands-off approach to sales that allows the customer freedom to browse, but allows them to reach out if they need help.

- NEVER abruptly leave a customer to greet another. Not only is it rude, the original customer may leave and never return.

  - However, you may excuse yourself momentarily to quickly greet the new customer to allow them to know who to reach out to if they require assistance.

- If you are assisting a customer and a telephone call interrupts, excuse yourself momentarily to answer the telephone.

<===[

- o If the call will take longer than a moment to resolve, hand it off to someone else and return to your customer. Otherwise, inform the caller that the organization is really busy and encourage them to visit.

- Unless otherwise indicated, answer the telephone in this manner:

  - o Thank you for calling ORGANIZATION'S NAME. This is YOUR FIRST NAME. How may I help you?

- ALWAYS Upsell.

  - o If someone is interested in a product, be it standing in an isle or at the register, recommend a companion product. Think of it like an add-on.

]===>

- If they are buying shoes, recommend a pair of socks.

- Unless you have the authority and you think that you can score a reluctant sale with a discount, clear it with a supervisor prior to making the offer.

- If you can accept a return, ensure that a second employee is involved in the process in case there is any dispute.

Ethical Concerns

Do not bribe, do not steal, do not peddle influence or information, do not intentionally hurt others and do not tread where you are not permitted. Other ethical concerns include:

- DO NOT except gifts from external sources unless otherwise indicated by your direct supervisor.

    o This includes offers of financial transactions and/or future employment.

- DO NOT misuse your title, authority or its resources.

- DO NOT engage in nepotism.

    o Nepotism can look bad to those outside of the organization as it can be perceived as favoritism, especially if two members of the same family or relationship are in the same

]===>

department.   It is even worse if one

supervises the other.

- In a family-ran organization, this rule

  need not apply.

- DO NOT engage in conflicts of interest.

  o Unless you have permission from a

    supervisor, it is preferred that you do not

    offer your time to another organization

    similar to this one while a member of this

    organization's staff.

    - If you feel that you have a conflict of

      interest, you will have 14 days to

      cease your involvement with either our

      organization or the other.

  o It is also preferred that you not engage in

    activities that will directly impair your ability

<===[

]==>

to function efficiently and effectively within

your obligation to the organization.   By

agreeing to work with us, you had agreed to

perform certain duties and meet certain

obligations to the best of your abilities.

<==[

Staff Relationships

While we cannot prevent members of the staff from becoming romantically involved, we do discourage it as a matter of morale and productivity. If the relationship were to negatively impact morale or productivity, we would have no choice but to either dismiss or transfer one, if not both participants in the relationship, from their current position(s).

]===>

Staff Meetings & Schedule

Periodically, there may be a mandatory meeting that will require that all staff attend. There should be at least 14 days of advanced notice so that staff members may plan ahead so that they may attend. If for any reason, notice is not given in at least 14 days in advance, it will be understandable if some cannot attend, however, repeated failure to attend the mandatory meetings given more than enough notice will result in dismissal. These meetings are important to the organization's success as well as your own.

Once your work schedule has been established, you must maintain regular attendance. Multiple missed days without finding a replacement or providing less than 24-hours of advanced notice will result in dismissal. If you think that you may be unable to make your scheduled shift for any reason, contact your direct

<==[

]===>
supervisor. They may assist you in coordinating your

replacement for the shift.

]==>
Staff Safety

Your safety as well as the safety of others is important to our organization. We strive to follow all applicable local, state and federal laws when it comes to your health in our workplace. We expect our employees to practice good safety habits by removing obstacles, returning items to where they belong and complying with all health and safety requirements where applicable.

It is illegal for those under the age of 18 years to load, unload or operate a trash compactor, per federal law.

]==>

Public Perception

The adage "any press is good press" is rather misleading. In the name of publicity, getting one's name out to the public for most reasons is a good thing. However, the press does not typically cover the good things that an organization does, unless it is a particularly slow news cycle. On the other hand, the adage that "no news is good news" implies that publicity is not one's goal. However, organizations must protect their image. How the public perceives them deeply impacts how well they will be able to function into the future.

We have gotten to the point where organizations need to protect themselves via non-disclosure agreements and policies that restrict public commentaries without prior approval. Many organizations suffer from disgruntled workers who

<==[

]===>
complain publicly about how the organization in which

they work because they are not allowed to do as they

would like. It may not seem to be worth much to the

organization as most complaints are simply an employee

venting, but this is how the rumor mill starts. A single

comment by an employee about being denied a larger

cubical can be misinterpreted into some rumor about

employees being locked in the office after hours and

unpaid until they finish their work.

In this day where social media is everywhere, a

number of organization actually run periodic checks via

search engines for Internet publicity. It is not unusual

for an organization to terminate someone for

insubordination because of the public comments they

made of an organization via the Internet that placed the

organization into a bad light. Frankly, if an organization

<===[

]===>

has so many internal issues where they must police the Internet to clear their name, maybe someone should look inwards for the reason as to why. If there are a particularly hefty number of complaints about the organization that are generally about the same problem, then it is quite obviously an internal issue that the organization needs to correct.

If any organization wishes to put in to place any public perception policies, it must be done in such a way where employees are given an advanced notice before enactment. This will allow them an opportunity to remove any previously made comments posted online and privatize any public social media accounts. These policies will also require employees to hold their tongues while in public, but cannot be enforced in one's home. If there is ever a negative comment made in the privacy of

<==[

]===>
one's home, whomever repeats it outside the home may

be made to suffer. If the individual does not work for

the organization, a defamation lawsuit, based upon

either libel or slander, may be the next logical step. Of

course, in this or any case, whatever is written or said

needs to make its way back to organization management

with proof to validate the claim.

One of the goals of any organization should be to

promote itself.   If organizations do not publicize

themselves, business will slow down. Never assume that

clientele or employees are promoting the organization.

Luckily, utilizing social media has a low cost of entry.

Setting up the bare minimum of social media accounts is

free and purchasing audience targeted advertising is

cost-effective. Most social media advertising allows for

the targeting of age groups, gender, locations and

<==[

]==>

related interests. The advertising saturation desired is entirely determined by the amount an organization is willing to spend. Cross-linking one's website with social media never hurts either.

<====================================[

]==>

Workplace Harassment

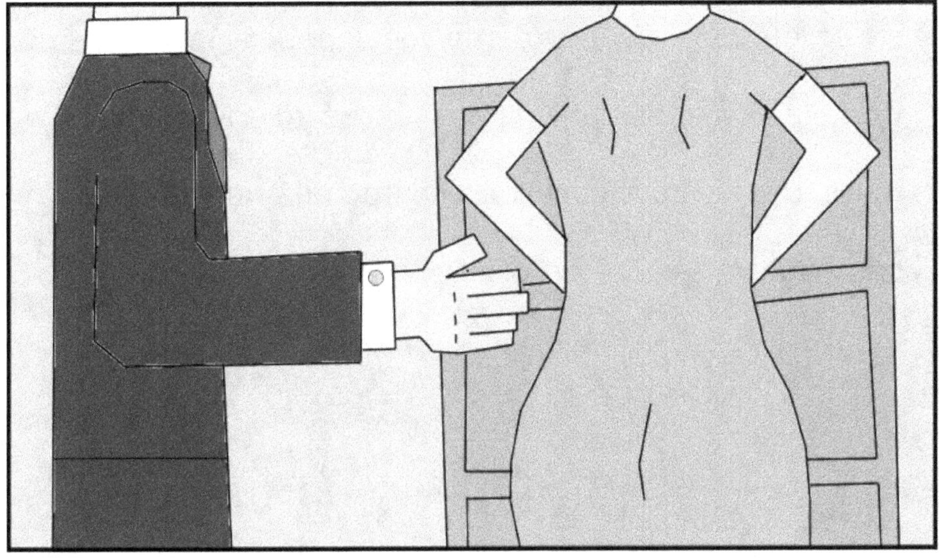

"Harassment of any type is a form of control. Control is any action that is used as a means to exert power over another against their permission. When people who desire control over another are rebuffed, it can sometimes lead to violence. It is no longer just men who harass women and with the glass ceiling broken in many places, women are just as capable of exerting control over others as men are." (Haslage, 2012, p. 22)

<==[

]==>
It is strictly prohibited to harass co-workers, be it on or off duty. Due to the legal nature involved with workplace harassment, it will not be tolerated and if we must, the authorities will be contacted and the offending parties dismissed.

<===[

Internet Bullying

While you may think that you are protected by Internet anonymity, you are not. A simple IP trace by someone knowledgeable in the use of Telnet protocols can trace where you are located to within a few feet. If you think that using your laptop or mobile device at a local coffee shop via their free WIFI will protect you, guess again. All devices that access the Internet have a MAC address. It can send information about your device, including your name and your telephone number in the case of cellular devices.

]===>

Sexual Harassment

Sexual harassment can happen when someone says or does something of a sexual nature, requests sexual favors or makes unwanted sexual advances. It does not matter if you are within a group of people of the same gender as your own, actions or discussions of a sexual nature will not be tolerated. This includes the display of sexual imagery and sound in your workspace, on your computer or on your mobile devices, while at the organization.

<===[

]===>
Versus Infatuation

Organizations in this era have begun implementing socialization policies in response to issues including sexual harassment, nepotism and other conflicts of interest. It makes sense in the financial long-run as social distractions of the aforementioned nature reduce efficiency in one way or another. That means money is not made as fast or as frequently when these issues arise.

The general complication that arises with nepotism occurs to others outside the relationship. When employees see another employee getting some type of perk because of their relationship to the boss, morale is reduced. The employees lose trust in the one receiving the perks and try to find ways to avoid working with them. Other conflicts of interest arise in such cases as where external relationships begin to get in the way of

<====================================[

]===>
business.   The most notable example is when an

employee is involved in a relationship with someone

from another organization that does business with their

own organization.   If the relationship ends badly, the

organizations may end up getting punished.

We have to keep in mind one very important thing

in all of this, we are human. We have emotions, feelings

and needs. Many of us prefer being loved and in love.

Sometimes it just happens that the person we are

interested in works with us.

It is a problem in our society now because a few

bad eggs have spoiled the bunch. People are either too

afraid to follow up on their emotions or do and go

overboard. However, for you romantics out there, there

is something you need to keep in mind.   You are not

committing sexual harassment if you ask a man or

<====================================[

]===>
woman out once in a calm and mature manner. No matter the answer, if you ask them only once and never again, it is not harassment. This means doing it in such a way as to not embarrass or insult them.

When someone asks someone else who works in the same organization out on a date, there is much to think about. Consider the socialization polices in place at the organization. If they say co-workers of the same department cannot be in a relationship, then there is a problem. If a relationship does occur, someone is going to need to be transferred or quit. Employee fraternization can be a slippery slope and organizations need to have policies written and in place to manage inter-office relationships.

For those looking for love, the best time and place to ask anyone out is usually at lunch, alone and in a

<==[

]==>

public place. This way they can have a conversation with witnesses outside of earshot. It provides a bit of mutual privacy and safety if things go awry. The worst that anyone can say in that situation is no. Someone may get their heart broken, but on the plus side it is not in the office where a spectacle can be made.

According to the Pew Research Center, as of 2019, 50 percent of all relationships start online. (Pew, 2020) There may eventually come a day where most office positions will be conducted via the Internet. Let us not fool ourselves because sexual harassment does and will still occur online. However, what the Internet does provide us is a bit of social courage. Some accredit it to anonymity, but frankly it has more to do with individuals being in their comfort zones.

<===[

]==>

Workplace Bullying

Any type of bullying involves a pattern of unwanted, negative actions that involves an imbalance of power or strength. We would like to think that we have hired mature adults who know the difference between appropriate and inappropriate behaviors with interacting with others, especially in the workplace.

<==[

]===>

Whistleblowing or "Tattle-Tailing"?

At a national call center in its customer service department, there is a policy of completing busy work when there are no telephone calls. If everything else is done, then personnel may find personal activities in which to occupy their time. In 2011, the day and evening shift personnel were relocated to the same office. Previous to this change, the shift workers never met, even though there was typically an overlap of two hours between the end of one shift and the start of another. The overlap was based upon how busy specific days of the week were between 3 and 5 p.m.

Within a week of the change in location, members of the day shift staff began submitting complaints against the evening shift staff that started at 3 p.m. The complaints typically revolved around evening shifters surfing the Internet or completing personal tasks at their

<==[

]===>
desks. Other minor complaints included evening shifters

completing busy work before day shifters and an issue

on how the office door should remain open or closed for

the sake of air circulation.

What was not being considered by the day shifters

was that they had a lot more work to do, thus they

rarely had free-time and this was reflected in how well

they were being paid. Plus, they were not getting paid

to complete the busy work as it was a low priority

normally handed by the evening shifters in the first place.

The argument on the placement of the door was the

result of a evening shifter's need to have the door

partially open due to a combination of germaphobia and

claustrophobia. In the previous evening shift office, the

staff had agreed to the door remaining half open.

However, no such agreement had been made in the new

<==[

]==>

combined office. When discussions were held on the topic, the day shifters refused to compromise.

The shift managers allowed the complaints to build up to the point that evening shifters who began at 3 p.m. stopped showing up to work. Eventually, the department manager called each office worker to their office individually and told each of them that they were adults, to stop acting like babies and to grow up. This ended up requiring the division manager to hold a departmental meeting pertaining to proper conduct in the workplace. As a result, realignment in the shift schedule was needed to decrease the chances of the affected evening shifters from being around the complaining day shifters.

The problem here is that we have two individuals that were accustomed to how things used to be and did

<==[

]===>
not take the time to understand the new situation. They

desired to negatively impact the new people in the office

so that perhaps they could return to a situation where

they felt more comfortable. These day shifters falsely

believed that if they complained enough, that they would

get their way. In this case, it worked, but it should not

have.   There   was   no   real   attempt   to   clarify   the

misunderstandings of the day shifters. If there had been

any   discussion,   perhaps   there   could   have   been   a

compromise where everyone would have been happier

with the results.

A "tattle-tail" likes to report on what someone else

is doing when they feel it may be unfair. In most of

these cases, what they feel is wrong may not necessarily

be wrong under the rules of the organization. In our

aforementioned case, the two individuals on day shift

<===[

]===>

were clearly comparing their situations to those people on the evening shift when they should not have been. The problem is, the organization never bothered to help anyone understand what the differences were and instead created a further divide in the staff.

Do not confuse a "tattle-tail" for a whistleblower. Whistleblowers are typically ethical individuals considering clear violations in organizational policy and perhaps even then law when they are reporting something of a questionable nature. The burden of proof rests in the hands of a whistleblower and the act alone can leave them open to ridicule, if not worse. The United States government has laws against retaliation of legitimate whistleblowers under the Whistleblower Protection Act of 1989. Illegitimate whistleblowers are typically those whom lie in an effort to receive some

<==[

]==>

benefit. Filing false whistleblowing reports can be illegal depending upon the nature.

The term ethical is used to define the legal standing in which a whistleblower can provide proof of another's illegal action. "Tattle-tails" are those who cite moral, non-legal reasons for why they feel something is unfair. To provide a little thought on the topic, ethics are to the law as morals are to opinion. Generally, ethics are objective where morals as subjective. In our society, we can be assured that the majority of us share similar ethical standards. However, morally the same cannot be said. To put it another way, ethics are what is right and wrong and morals are what is good and bad.

The typical procedure for handling "tattle-tails" is for management to inform them of the rules that they clearly do not seem to understand. The typical

<==[

]===>

procedure for handling whistleblowers is for management to inform them that the burden of proof is theirs to bear and that they must follow the chain of command when reporting. Never report directly to the individual in whom a complaint is against, go to their immediate supervisor.

The ability of whistleblowers to see and report unethical, and perhaps even illegal, behavior assists us in keeping our society safe from overwhelming corruption. As administrators, we must be able to tell the different between tattle-tails and whistleblowers and thus must encourage open dialog for when complaints arise.

So when does whistle-blowing come into play? There are a number of reasons to blow the whistle on someone. The primary reasons normally include criminal

<===[

]===>
offenses such as bribery, collusion, fraud or theft.

Another good reason is when there is danger to the

health and safety of any individual or the failure to

comply with applicable legal and contractual obligations.

Disclosing private or privileged information without

permission can be a means for both civil and legal

prosecution.   On an inclusive level, there is the

deliberate concealment of information about any of the

aforementioned items. If someone is issuing a complaint

and one of the aforementioned reasons is not why, then

there may need to be a reassessment on the action to be

taken.

<=======================================[

]===>

Conflict Resolution

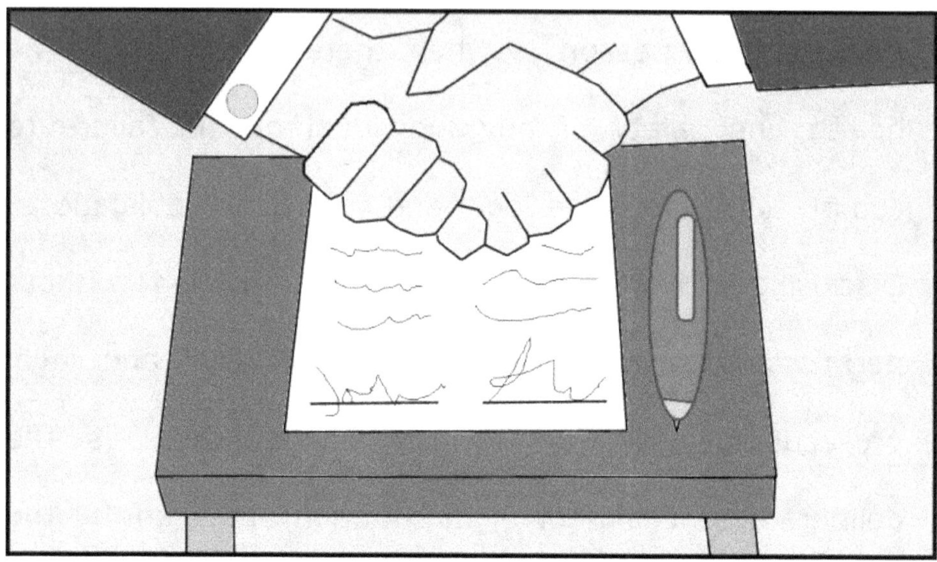

Ulysses S. Grant once coined the phrase, "good help is hard to find these days". In many types of jobs, that is a very true statement. In positions where special skills are needed, finding suitable replacements is a rather difficult task. Many managers can say that they have experienced an occasion where one employee did not get along with another.

]==>

Most of the time when two employees do not seem to get along, it is due to a simple misunderstanding. It is often the case where the particular reason may be important to one and not to the other. The employee who is offended ignores the other and in turn the other ignores them back without really knowing why they are being ignored in the first place. Ignoring each other will not last forever. Sometimes the issue resolves itself, but when it does not violence may be the next action taken. It is the job of the manager to identify when an issue may be brewing and put a stop to it.

If it gets to the point where the dislike between two employees becomes disruptive or violent, mediation will be required. Mediation is required for the sake of the bottom line and to reduce liability. Plus, happy employees are usually good employees.

<==[

]==>

The most common type of mediation is the neutral third-party method. An individual acting in the best interest of both parties encourages conversation to locate and resolve the issue at hand while keeping the employees on task. This method requires time to be spent dedicated to rooting out the issues and should never be forced. Forcing an outcome still leaves the employees with feelings of the issue still remaining unresolved and will eventually return the situation back to where it was prior to the mediation.

<===[

]==>
The Cost of Mediation

A forced mediation never works. However, no organization should ever spend too much precious time or money on mediation unless the employees are extremely difficult to replace. Consider the cost of mediation versus replacement.

First, how long has the issue between the employers been occurring? Does the issue affect non-involved employees? Has there been a noticeable loss in production? If the loss can be framed in monetary terms, how much is it? The monetary amount conceived is the cost of the employees not getting along.

Second, now consider how much it would cost to replace both of the employees. This includes the hiring process and training. Does the cost of the employees not getting along exceed the cost of replacing them? If

<==[

]==>

so, then too much time has been spent allowing these employees disrupt the work place.

A decision needs to be made and action needs to be taken now. Either arrange for mediation or hire new employees. It is a gamble as both mediation and new employees are not guaranteed to work out. There is no way to recoup the financial losses, but perhaps they can be reduced in the short-term and something can be learned to reduce the chances of this happening again.

<==[

]===>

Step-by-Step Mediation

Authors Douglas Stone, Bruce Patton and Sheila Heen's "Difficult Conversations" is a great guide for mediation (Stone, 1999). While it focuses on one-on-one mediation, it is not impeded by having a neutral third party making sure everyone stays on task and revealing the important points. It is a good read for any manager who may have to handle employee relationship issues. Going step-by-step and based off these author's work, I will break down the important points and add a few additions of my own.

Step 1: Define the problem

There are three conversations going on whenever there is an issue between two individuals. The first is based on the view of the first employee. The second is based on the view of the second employee. The third is the conversation of both employees combined that

<===[

]===>

provide the real story. The job of the mediator is to see what is common between the views and reveal it.

"When competent, sensible people do something stupid, the smartest move is to try to figure out, first, what kept them from seeing it coming and second, how to prevent the problem from happening again." (Stone, p. 12)

Step 2: Stop arguing about whom is right

We are individuals with freewill and our own view the world different from one and another. What you see is not necessarily what I see. "Often we go through an entire conversation – on indeed an entire relationship – without ever realizing that each of us is paying attention to different things, that our views are based on different information." (Stone, p. 32-3) We often hold

<==[

]==>
conversations with each other and what one person may

think is benign another may take offense.

Step 3: Do not assign intent where none may exist

"Much of the first mistake can be traced to one

basic error: we make an attribution about another

person's intentions based on the impact of their actions

on us." (Stone, p. 46) In this age of technology, we

sometimes cannot help ourselves when it comes to

placing intent on the messages we receive. If we would

take the time to ask if there was any intent involved

before making accusations, a whole lot of trouble could

be avoided.

"Interestingly, when people take on the job of

thinking hard about their own intentions, it sends a

profoundly positive message to the other person about

the importance of the relationship. After all, you'd only

<===[

]==>

do that kind of hard work for somebody who matters to you." (Stone, p. 52).

Step 4: Abandon blame

A lot of time in mediation is wasted by playing the blame game. This deviation from the task at hand can easily escalate in a negative way and needs to be avoided. "The urge to blame is based, quite literally, on a misunderstanding of what has given rise to the issues between you and another person, and on that fear of being blamed." (Stone, p. 59)

Step 5: The sharing of feelings

This is perhaps one of the more difficult parts of mediation, mainly in the case of men. Men try a little too hard to conceal how they really feel and often times it erupts into an explosion of negative emotion. "Beginning with 'I feel...' is a simple act that carries with it extraordinary benefits. It keeps the focus on feelings

<==[

]===>
and makes clear that you are speaking only from your

perspective." (Stone, p. 105)

To encourage a discussion of feelings, it is a good

idea to ensure them that it is a safe place to do so.

However, it must be made clear that no one will have

the right to ridicule another about exposing how they

really feel.

Step 6: What is at stake?

For the employer, what is at stake is lost time and

money. For the employees, it may be their income.

There is a lot depending on a positive outcome of

mediation. The key is making sure that the employees

know what is at risk if they do not take mediation

seriously.

"The more easily you can admit to your own

mistakes, your own mixed emotions, and your own

<=================================[

]===>

contributions to the problem, the more balanced you will

feel during the conversation and the higher the chance it

will go well." (Stone, p. 119)

Step 7: Individual goals

Everyone usually has some predetermined goal

when getting involved in mediation. The mediator wants

a fair resolution and the employees involved want to feel

vindicated. "The gold standard here is working for

mutual understanding. Not [a] mutual agreement,

necessarily, but a better understanding of each of your

stories, so that you can make informed decisions (alone

or together) about what to do next." (Stone, p. 145)

"Letting them know up front that your goal for the

discussion is to understand their perspective better,

share your own, and talk about how to go forward

<===[

]==>

together makes the conversation significantly less mysterious and threatening." (Stone, p. 155)

Step 8: Listening

While an employee reveals their story and feelings, the other should be listening intently. "Listening well is one of the most powerful skills you can bring to a difficult conversation. It helps you understand that other person. And, importantly, it helps them understand you." (Stone, p. 163)

Step 9: Paraphrasing

Upon the completion of a story, to show that they were in fact listening, the other employee should paraphrase what was said. "First, paraphrasing gives you a chance to check your understanding... Second, paraphrasing lets the other person know they've been heard." (Stone, p. 179)

<==[

]===>

Step 10: Resolution

"Difficult conversations require a certain amount of compromise and mutual accommodation to the other's needs." (Stone, p. 210) Both employees need to be able to agree on a resolution. Often times the practice of simply discussing the issue reveals its own truths and solution. Mediation is a means to an end when it comes to convincing two parties that a discussion is past due.

"Generally the best way to manage conflict in a way that safeguards a relationship is to look for standards or fair principles to guide a resolution, rather than trying to haggle with or intimidate the other person. If you can't find a creative way to solve the problem, ask what standards of fairness should apply, and why." (Stone, p. 214)

The end result may not necessarily be the result everyone initially had in mind, but unless the worst

<==[

]===>

possible situation of a non-resolution occurred, everyone

should feel a little better about the outcome and can get

back to work.

<===[

]===>

Staff Appearance & Behavior

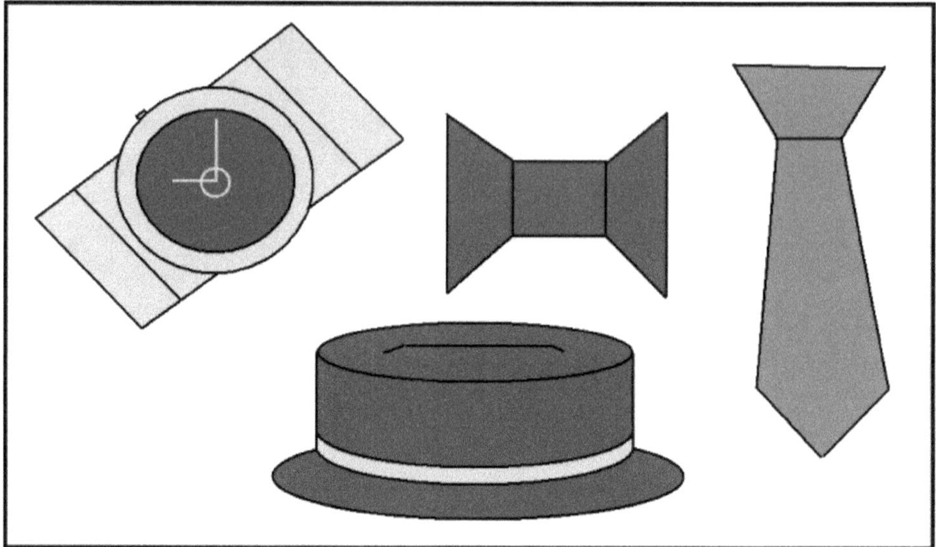

You are expected to be neatly groomed and

lacking of any offensive odors. As a representative of

this organization, your appearance and behavior impacts

a customer's level of satisfaction.

<=======================================[

Dress Code

Unless clothing is provided to you by the organization, you are expected to wear outfits that are clean and free of defect that are appropriate for the work that you will be completing. As a general rule, it is encouraged that you wear the appropriate clothing to meet the situation:

Casual Dress

- Dresses – Short or long-sleeved, just above knee-length, pocketed or not, loose fitting, belted or string-tied. Nothing that exposes any part of the chest.

- Over-shirt – Short or long-sleeved, pocketed or not, loose fitting, collared, capable of being fully buttoned or zipped and tucked-in.

- Pants – Belted or buttoned, anything but tight fit.

]==>

- Shoes – Appropriate for the surface that you will be treading upon as well as the distance that you will be travelling. Black, non-slip shoes are generally preferred.

- Shorts – Just above knee-length, pocketed or not, loose fitting, belted or string-tied.

- T-shirts – Short or long-sleeved, pocketed or not, loose fitting, revealing no more than an inch around the neckline and capable of bring tucked-in.

Formal Dress

- Dress Coats – Long sleeved, pocketed or not and loose fitting (if not custom tailored).

- Dress Shirts – Short or long-sleeved, pocketed or not, loose fitting, collared and capable of being tucked in.

<===[

]===>

- Dresses – Short or long-sleeved, just above knee-length, pocketed or not, loose fitting, belted or string-tied. Nothing that exposes any part of the chest.

- Neck Tie – If you find yourself wearing a dress shirt that will be tucked in, wear a neck tie. It should have a tie clip to keep it from getting in the way.

- Shoes – Dress shoes.

- Slacks – Belted or buttoned, anything but tight fit.

The outfit that you wear for a formal meeting should match the atmosphere of that meeting, thus if everyone else will be wearing a suit and tie, you should be wearing them as well.

<==[

]===>

Accessories & Decorations

When it comes to wearing accessories such as bracelets, necklaces, rings and watches, a conservative approach is best. That same is true about dying one's hair, painting one's nails and tattoos. However, exceptions must be permitted under the requirements of religious doctrine. The only exception is when they pose an inherit safety risk, such as in the case of operating machinery. The following is a list of general rules:

- Avoid dangling earrings, studded earrings are generally acceptable.

- Limit jewelry to a single item per location, such as only one bracelet, one necklace, one earring per ear, one ring per finger (except the "ring" finger) and so on.

- All jewelry and tattoos must be able to be easily concealed by clothing.

<===[

]===>

- o An unexpected occasion may require a more professional setting where jewelry and tattoos will need to be quickly hidden.

- Less vibrant the color of one's hair and finger nails, the more professional it seems.

- Hair must be neatly groomed.

- o If the hair is long, it must either be tied back or stylized, such as in a bun.

- Facial hair must be either clean-shaven or neatly trimmed.

Staff Identification

Depending upon the activity that the organization has assigned you, you may be required to wear some form of identification. The primary reason that you would need to visibly wear identification is when dealing with customers. It is considered a sign of being friendly

<==[

]==>

and approachable if a customer can call you by name.

Another reason may be when you are working with a

new supervisor and they wish to learn everyone's name.

The most important reason is for security. Sometimes

identification is the only way anyone will know who

belongs where within the organization and its property.

The most common form of identification is badges

via clip-ons and/or lanyards. Some badges can be

simple and printed from a computer while others can

contain a computer chip that grants access to certain

doors. Then again, some badges are made of plastic and

have a magnetic strip on the back that requires the staff

member to write their name with a dry-erase marker on

it each day. One day, badges may even contain a two-

way radio activated by a simple tap.

<===[

]===>
Behavioral Expectations

It is expected that staff members are mature enough to be self-reliant, enabling the organization to operate as efficiently and trouble-free as possible. However, we also need staff to be able to be comfortable enough to inform a direct supervisor when there is an issue. Specifically, we need you to do the following:

- Report illegal, suspicious or unethical conduct by customers and staff.

- Cooperate with any investigation by the organization and outside authorities.

- Eat meals outside of the view of customers.

- If you require a break, make sure that someone else will cover your assignment while you are away.

- Comply with all policies and procedures as highlighted in this document and distributed

<==[

]==>

around the organization. Failure to do so may

result in dismissal.

<====================================[

Political Correctness

Political correctness is a means to remove the emotions elicited from language as a method of returning to a polite society. Many people are capable of accepting common language in the context transmitted, but others are sensitive to the specific parts of the message. There is also the matter of a word or phrase meaning one thing for one person and meaning something entirely different for another. Political correctness attempts to kill two birds with one stone, but exists without considering each individual's ability to comprehend any language at the same level as another.

For example, not everyone speaks English, is born in the Great Lakes region of the mid-western United States and have a graduate degree in literature. The aforementioned factors provide a different level of language comprehension compared to an English

]==>
speaking farmer with no formal education growing corn

in Iowa. The farmer is not an unintelligent man by any

means, but political correctness means nothing to him

and if used while spoken to him, he may respond with a

puzzled look. He may also respond negatively for talking

up to him or be insulted for talking down to him when

trying to explain what was meant.

The emotions spoken of in language consist of the

words that elicit them. Of course ethnic, racial, sexual

and other slurs upset some people. For other people,

slurs are slang with no more meaning than the word

they replace. Some words considered to be curse-words,

as well as many slurs, are now used as nouns and verbs

meant to replace more polite language. However, if we

consider the feelings of others before we communicate

<===[

]==>

and say what we mean, political correctness is

unnecessary.

]==>
# General Ethical Concerns

Sometimes people confuse ethics and morals. For many people, they are the same thing, but in actuality they help us build our belief system. Ethics are objective beliefs while morals are subjective beliefs. Ethics are usually inherit to the laws of a community and are the same amongst its members while morals are opinions that one person decides upon for themselves based upon information learned from a combination of resources. To

<==[

]==>

state it simply, ethics define right and wrong while morals determine good and bad.

Ethically, we know that it is illegal to steal bread, thus we also know that stealing bread is wrong. Morally, we also know that it is bad to steal bread, but it is good to steal bread if someone would die without the bread. In certain circumstances, as shown in the previous example, sometimes we ignore either ethics in favor or morality. However, the situation is that we live in a community where the law has more weight than our beliefs. Thus, ethics must be the overriding basis for all decision making, even if one's morals suggest otherwise. Ultimately, ethical decisions protect the organization in addition to yourself or others.

<==[

Accepting & Receiving Gifts

It is almost always a bad idea to accept gifts from external sources. From the outside, it may be seen as some type of bribe. The exceptions to the rule are the results of cultural traditions. In many Asian cultures, the exchange of gifts is customary prior to the discussion of business. In certain parts of the world, it is common practice to send gifts to someone who has provided some type of assistance as a thank you.

Gift giving is not necessarily safe internally either. Gifts between co-workers for birthdays or holidays do not typically raise eyebrows, but gifts exchanged between a supervisor and subordinate may be seen as there is some type of impropriety occurring.

When a gift exchange does occur in the workplace, it is encouraged that gifts not exceed 25 dollars in market value. Those above the specified amount should

]===>

be returned with a polite letter as to why it is being

returned. For whom gifts are exchanged outside of the

workplace, provided they are not with those in which

they conduct business officially, are their own concern.

For example, receiving a gift from a relative is

acceptable. Receiving a gift from a co-worker who

socializes outside of work is also acceptable. Receiving a

gift from a co-worker at work must be done according to

workplace policies. However, receiving a gift from a

contractor that is associated with the workplace is not

acceptable.

The simple lesson is if the gifts, be they financial

or otherwise, are in any way related to the workplace,

follow the rules. Although, if you do not wish to or

cannot keep a gift and are unable to return it, donate it

<===[

]==>
to a worthy cause. Just remember to get a receipt as

proof of the donation.

<==[

]===>

Conflicts of Interest

A conflict of interest can occur in any number of ways, the most common being compensation and employment. For this discussion, compensation does not necessary mean only pay, it means any financial gain. For example, trading privileged information for compensation is highly unethical. If it is done to gain an edge in the financial markets, it is a felony known as insider trading.

The term "moonlighting" means to hold a second job. Back in the age when most jobs were 9 a.m. to 5 p.m., those who had a second job had them at night and were called "moonlighters."

Conflicts of interest in employment arise when what occurs on one job directly impacts the other. For example, it is never a good idea to work for two companies that are in direct competition. It is worse if

<==[

]===>

the positions held in both companies are high level

administration. From both sides of the argument, it can

be argued that someone is using information they garner

from each company to seek some type of gain, be it

financial or otherwise. It can also be seen as corporate

spying, no matter if any wrongdoing was actually being

conducted.

Another conflict of interest in employment, though

rare, is working for both a company and its subsidiary.

Not every company is comfortable with employees

working for both a parent and child company. Primarily,

an issue within one position could impact the other.

Otherwise, it becomes a concern when someone has

competing interests or gains insider knowledge that

could be used in the other position. It could become a

slippery slope.

<==[

]===>

Misuse of Position & Resources

To misuse one's position is the misuse of one's name, title and authority. To provide an official quote when not authorized, utilizing the job title for perks or using one's authority to get one's way is very unethical. Stan Lee said frequently that "with great power comes great responsibility." It is a valuable lesson to learn, one that has been with us since the origins of the Bible.

No matter where one works, it is never a good idea to use workplace resources for personal reasons. There are some limited exceptions that each place may permit, but performing external business at any workplace should be frowned upon.

<===[

]===>

Nepotism

Historically, nepotism occurs between friends and relatives at the workplace. Perhaps a brother lands a job, talks up his sister and now she is working there too. Other times, it is a couple, married or otherwise, who may or may not have first met at the workplace. Where the problems normally occur is when one becomes a direct supervisor of another.

Nepotism smacks of impropriety without even trying. Those on the outside looking in always see favoritism being played, even when there is none. However, there is also the issue of drama from home finding its way to work. Plus, it could potentially ruin relationships and disrupt business. It is always best to avoid this situation and if necessary, assign someone to another department.

<==[

```
]=============================================>
```

Shrinkage

You may have heard of this term before. This is the term used when inventory or money goes missing. As you may know, nothing is free and when someone steals or something gets misplaced, the organization loses money. If enough ends up disappearing, the organization will also disappear.

Loss Prevention (LP)

The following are ways that staff can help the organization prevent a loss of inventory and money:

- NEVER leave a customer waiting.
- NEVER face away from the sales floor for too long.
- Know how to covertly alert a supervisor of a suspected crime in progress.
  - NEVER take your eye off of a suspected thief until your supervisor says otherwise.

```
<=============================================[
```

]===>

- ONLY law enforcement or security should detain suspected thieves.
  - NEVER chase after a suspected thief as you never know if they have a weapon, plus falsely accusing someone could be embarrassing and bad for business.
- ALWAYS check an area once a customer has vacated it to ensure that it is in order.
  - If there are clothes for sale, this is an opportunity to check for empty hangers.
- ALWAYS keep the sales floor, particularly the register area, clean and organized.
- ALWAYS keep the location of all security systems confidential.
- ALWAYS report suspected losses to a supervisor.

<==[

]===>

We would like to believe that everyone that we hire has the best intentions, but sometimes that is not always the case. It would be ignorant of our organization to not consider that some loss is internal. The following list is how we can combat internal shrinkage, some of which can result in legal action:

- Staff must enter and leave the organization through the staff door, if available.
  - Staff property is subject to inspection upon entrance and exit.
- Staff must make their purchases on their own time.
  - Staff purchases must be processed by a supervisor.
    - This includes purchases for and by staff family members using staff discounts and memberships.

<==[

]==>

- All bank transactions require that two staff members be involved at all times.

  o This includes from counting down the drawer to the bank deposit.

- DO NOT use another staff member's assigned equipment without a supervisor's permission.

- Unauthorized entities are not permitted in staff areas.

- DO NOT engage in these activities else face instant dismissal:

  o Falsification of organization records

  o Giving keys/card access to the organization to unauthorized entities

  o Hacking of organization computer information systems

  o Leaving the organization without permission

<==[

]==>

- o Theft from the organization or each other

- o Trespassing on organization property after

  hours, without permission

- o Vandalism of organization property

<==[

]===>
Other Definitions

- Bribery – "The illegal acceptance of money or other valuable considerations in exchange for special favors from public servants having to do with their official duties." (Cooper, p. 136)

- Influence Peddling – "When a public employee attempts to influence a governmental decision in favor of a third party in which the employee has an interest." (Cooper, p. 137)

- Information Peddling – "Officials who are privy to information not available to the general public and use it to their own advantage, monetary or otherwise." Think of it like insider trading. (Cooper, p. 137)

- Financial Transactions – "When a public servant has direct or indirect financial interest that directly conflict

<===[

]===>

with the responsible performance of the job."
(Cooper, p. 138)

- Gifts and Entertainment – This is a form of bribery.

- Outside Employment – "Part-time employment, consulting, contractual retainers, and self-employment" that utilizes governmental employment status as a means to garner work and may also use governmental property to assist in that work. This is also known as double-dipping. (Cooper, p. 138)

- Future Employment – "If a public employee intends to seek employment in the future with a firm he or she now transacts official business with, the tendency may be to give favored treatment to this prospective employer in hopes of encouraging a job offer." (Cooper, p. 139)

<===[

Other Concerns

From pay to violence in the workplace, certain statements are required to be made that ensure no one has an excuse in legitimizing negative actions.

]===>
Businesses Are Not Democracies

One could choose to provide opportunities to employees to vote on small parts of how the business is operated. In doing so, it would give them a better sense of being a part of something bigger than just a cog in the machine. However, the business cannot operate as a Democracy unless employees are also provided some form of ownership in the business. Businesses are operated with a plan in mind and may have shareholder investment and returns to consider. An employee is not typically terminated if a quarterly goal is not met. It is the big cheese that the board of directors relieves. However, offering ownership to all employed provides them with personal stakes in the investment of the organization.

<====================================[

]===>
Paydays & Tax Forms

If you have been hired to fill a paid position, you may be expected to complete an I-9 (Employment Eligibility Verification) and a W-4 (Withholding Allowance Certificate) form. Periodically, you will get paid for your service. Depending upon the options available, be it cash card, check or direct deposit, you are expected to set one of those up prior to your first pay period, else you will be paid via the default method.

<======================================[

]===>
Parking

The parking closest to the organization should be for the customers. Unless there is employee specific parking or you have a disability that prevents you from walking the distance, park as far as you can from the organization within its parking area.

Smoking, Drinking & Illicit Narcotic Use

Smoking, no matter the product, drinking alcohol and using illicit drugs are strictly prohibited. In addition, it is illegal to do so near and inside of most organizations in most states. If a staff member is discovered partaking in any of these substances on the organization's property, they will have no choice but to dismiss them.

]===>
Violence & Firearms

Violence of any type is not permitted on the organization's property or with other staff members off of its property. Violation of this policy will not only require the involvement of law enforcement, but result in your dismissal.

Unless you are law enforcement or security with the proper licensing, you should not have a weapon on the organization's property. If you are discovered with a weapon, you will be removed from the premises by law enforcement and dismissed.

<===[

]===>

Internet Access

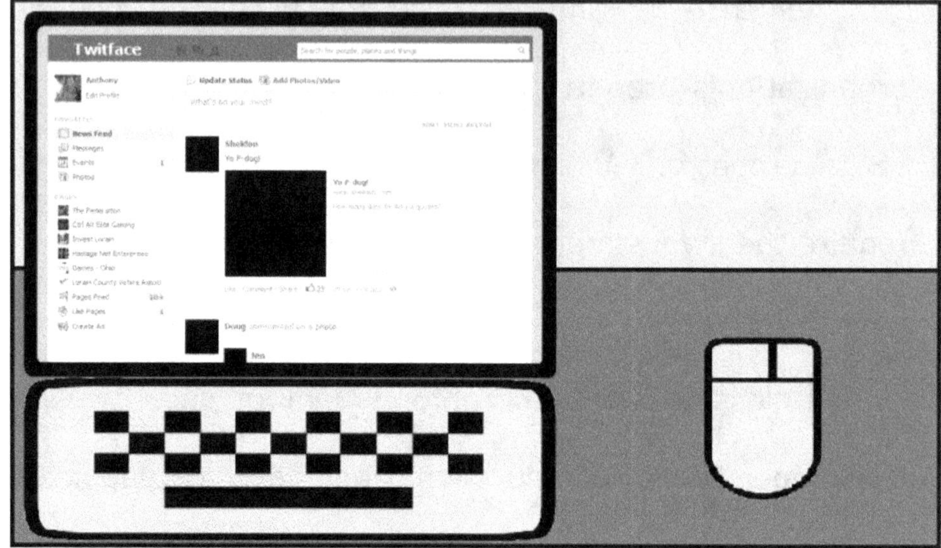

While you are at the organization and using its Internet, your communications may be recorded and reviewed for security purposes. It is discouraged that staff utilize the Internet for personal reasons as doing do only results in reduced productivity. If it is discovered that a staff member is using the Internet for personal reasons without permission, they will initially lose access. Repeated abuse will result in dismissal.

<===[

Social Media

As you know, all organizations are open to ridicule. Be it from the employees, volunteers, the public or people not even served by the organization. We have all heard the sayings that "any press is good press" and that "the word of mouth is the best type of advertising." The fact is that it really depends on the message.

We live in an age where computers are freely accessible in many places and as of the year 2020, approximately 97 percent of the American population owns a cellular telephone. (Pew, 2021) Most cellular telephones are little computers in themselves. After the year 2010, the chance of buying a new cellular telephone that simply makes calls and nothing more became difficult. Sure, there are those models tailored towards small children and the elderly with the large buttons that

]===>

auto-dial a few pre-programmed numbers, but those normally require a visit to a specialty store or website.

Keeping the aforementioned children and elderly exception aside, including those individuals who are not technologically savvy or socially compatible, let us consider who is the average web surfer. Generally, in the United States a web surfer is someone between the ages of 10 and 55 with frequent access to a computer or a cellular telephone. Most people with a computer have a cellular telephone, not the other way around. Most office professionals have multiple computers, cellular telephones or other similar devices. They divide technology between private life and work. Students have access to technology in class and at home, even if in some cases it is against policy.

<====================================[

]==>

The process of logging in to the Internet to check how everyone else is doing has become so easy that there are actual addictions in existence to describe those too "plugged in." Social media in the last two decades has made our planet seem like a much smaller place. Almost no matter where Americans are, they can quickly post a status update, send a message to someone, and even post photos and videos online.

This era of Internet connectivity has both positive and negative consequences for any organization. On the positive, good promotion is appreciated and sometimes is a great help. On the negative, bad promotion can destroy an organization. You never hear about the lives saved by some charities day to day, but you sure do hear about when a member of management quits expectantly after some comments they made online

<====================================[

]===>

were discovered. During the year 2011, a few countries had their governments trembling from the efforts of Internet savvy citizenry who gathered many in a common cause. The end results in a few cases were the government leaders being overthrown.

After discussions with a number of organization managers and their employees, there are a few conclusions that most parties can get behind. First, employees should be encouraged to promote the positive efforts of the organization via the Internet and report the problems to management. Second, the organization should engage in periodic checks for problems via the Internet. Third, organizations should create a simple policy, perhaps a line in its code of conduct, that prohibits public displays of negative behavior or

<==[

]===>
comments in reference to the organization in public and online, else face penalties.

In this age of identity theft, the smartest amongst us prohibit access to online profiles by strangers and the unapproved. It is a great policy to have and because of the privacy they enjoy, individuals have used social media to bemoan or gripe about their job and it is their right to do so. It is a nice way to alleviate stress. What is being said is not public and it is in this case that the organization should not care.   The organization's management should not also attempt to befriend employees via social media unless they plan to toss organizational policy out the window.   If you are befriended, it is assumed they are befriending you, not the organization and they expect their private thoughts

<===[

]===>
shared with you and their other friends to be just that,

private.

Again, if the profile is accessible to the public, then that is when policy can be enacted. The reason for this separation of what is allowed and not otherwise is simply to reduce effort and ease minds. Plus, the argument of where the freedom of speech fits in is protected in private conversations better than publicly. Hearsay is not admissible in court, so that means that unless the organization's management can hear or see something about them while acting on behalf of the organization, there is little they can do.

In this era of social media, we are generally much more social than we have ever been. The difference between us now and 20 years ago is that we do not have to leave the home to complain to our friends about work.

<===[

]===>
Sure, we have telephones and the invention of three-way calling was nice, but now we can potentially complain to a countless number of friends all at one time. As it is, potential and current employers do read employee Facebook pages and Twitter feeds. When people befriend their bosses online, in most cases, those bosses are obligated to report disturbing issues to others and that can impact one's job status. That is why those in human resource management tell supervisors to avoid social interactions outside of work with subordinates. If they do befriend subordinates, a day will come when they have to choose a friend or loyalty to the job. More often than not, the job will come first and the friend will be jobless. This has been a common occurrence in the last 15 years.

<==[

]===>
Website Management Agreement

If you accept a social media or website

management role with this organization, you agree to

use the abilities that are given to you solely for the

purpose of promoting the agreed upon activities and/or

products. You also agree to not adjust the settings of

the social media or website(s) without the permission of

your direct supervisor. In addition, you agree not to

alter or delete materials submitted by other managers

and will report any questionable materials to your direct

supervisor. However, you are permitted to respond to

public requests for information if you feel that you

qualified to respond as well as remove any publicly

submitted materials if the content can be considered

questionable. It is further noted that all posted content

must be family-friendly and placed only in the

designated locations. Any violation of this agreement

<==[

]==>
will result at minimum in your removal from the

management role and/or at maximum in legal action,

depending upon the severity of the infraction.

<====================================[

]===>

Community Service

In 2013, David A. Kelly was at Lorain County Community College where he led a presentation based upon his book, "The Courage to Serve," as part of a student leadership event. The presentation primarily focuses on the efforts of servant leaders and the author believes that many organizations can learn from what Kelly teaches. We will be using as much of the presentation's content as possible while adapting it

<===[

]===>

accordingly so that it may better fit the needs of many different types of organizations. This adaptation has been made with permission. For more information on Kelly's work, you may contact him via e-mail (DaveKelly@GonzoSpeaks.com), telephone (770-552-6592) or visit his website (http://www.gonzospeaks.com/). (Kelly, 2013)

Introduction

Have you ever seen an opportunity for your organization to serve and avoided it? If you did not avoid it, did you ever ignore it? Was it out of fear? Service is a zero-sum game after all. You put a piece of your organization out there to help someone else and they may reject your overture or worse yet, take advantage of the organization. You rarely get a positive

<===[

]==>

return from your organization's service efforts, so why

bother?

You should bother because we are all called to

serve.   Throughout American history, our greatest

politicians and leaders have given much of themselves to

serve others. Benjamin Franklin, a well-known inventor

and publisher, got involved in politics when he saw it

was time for American independence from England.

Abraham Lincoln was a jack-of-all-trades who eventually

became a lawyer before becoming the President that

fought to end slavery and reunite our nation.   Martin

Luther King Jr. grew up in the segregated south and

fought for equal civil rights.   There are countless other

examples of servant leaders throughout our history.

To top it off, a number of modern day

organizations utilize plenty of resources for good causes.

<==[

]===>
Perhaps the best example may be the Bill & Melinda Gates Foundation. The Gates Foundation donates a large sum of money and technical know-how each year to educational institutes to update technology. They also provide the means to feed and inoculate large populations within third-world countries.

Service is innate within our being. So, why is it such a hard thing to do? Because society is telling us to "Just Do It" and get ours. We have many demands on our time and sometimes it is hard to go to those places where people need to be served. The thing is, finding a place to serve does not have to be difficult. Consider the ground at your feet, the community around where your organization is based.

Certain organizations have a stigma placed upon them about being purely focused on a single goal,

<===[

]===>
making money. Make money for the owners, investors

and employees, but not for the surrounding community.

While historically, having such a narrow-minded focus

has made many people rich, it has never lasted very

long without the help of the community-at-large.

Eventually, your organization's patrons will notice what

your organization is and is not doing and the end results

can either be potentially advantageous or disastrous.

Getting involved in the community does not have to

make them money, it just needs to show that your

organization is part of the community and it understands

that the community's success is its success and visa-

verse.

"I spoke at the U.S. Coast Guard Academy in the

fall of 2007, in New London, Connecticut," said Kelly,

"After the program, one of the cadets offered to take me

<====================================[

]==>

on a tour of the facility. She was Second Class Cadet

Tory Stevens… As we went on the tour, Tory would

periodically stop and almost ritualistically, as if at

attention, reach down and pick up pieces of garbage and

put them in her pocket. After she had done it several

times, I finally asked her if this was something that was

expected of her as a cadet, something that was part of

the honor code." Stevens responds, "Oh no, I have

always done this. I figure if I pick up at least one piece

of garbage per day, then that means that there will be

365 less pieces of garbage in the world every year."

Your organization is not being asked to sponsor

some third-world country. But, do you have the courage

to encourage service on a daily basis? So, what can

your organization do? Will your organization make a

commitment to be like Tory Stevens? Can your

<===[

]===>

organization serve in quiet? When you see a need, will your organization step up? If you can do that once every day for a year, how much better will the world be? Call it the Servant 365 Project. There are a few things that you need to know, however. There is no website or blog for this, there are no forms to fill our or dues to pay, and there will be probably very little glory for you, unless you can get some love via social media. But you will feel difference and the example that you set may influence someone else to do something even bigger.

The courage to serve requires each individual to step outside of themselves. Just a little and sometimes, just a little bit more. There will also be times when your organization will have to separate itself from the crowd. The courage to serve is also about developing a lifetime commitment to serving others. That can start no matter

<===[

]==>

where your organization is based, how big it may be and no matter how old it is.

On the individual level, service to others can grow and develop into servant leadership. Modern day leaders of this movement believe that true leadership emanates from serving others. If anyone comes to leadership in any other way, then they are coming from a point of "me first" rather than "others first." As a servant leader, one puts themselves out there, maybe getting out of their comfort zone, and demonstrating that they are willing to put the organization first. In doing so, they rise to a level of responsibility and leadership because people trust them and they see within them the heart of a servant.

This leads them and you to the most courageous thing of all: becoming a leader. The courage to serve

<==[

]==>
includes leading others. Does your staff have the courage to take on a leadership role? Is this something that your organization wants? Is it something that is being thrust upon them? Ready or not, here are five tips to help your staff become a better leader and to have the courage to serve others.

Tip One: Get outside of your comfort zone.

Everyone needs to toss aside their own egos and concerns about what people will think about them and get involved. No one should concern themselves with being rejected.

Tip Two: Little things mean a lot.

Small efforts at service can make such a huge difference for other people, like the cadet picking up trash and the insurance company commercials that shows a positive chain reaction of small acts of service.

<===[

]===>

Tip Three: Begin with the baby steps.

You, your organization or its staff may want to save the world, but do not get overwhelmed. While it is important to make community service a habit, start out with small efforts that do not require a lot of planning or even a lot of people to complete. There are many things that most anyone can do, such as reading to elementary school kids, tutoring, picking up trash, visiting animal shelters to play with and exercise the animals or visit a nursing home.

When everyone is ready to take on something a little bit bigger, there are usually local agencies that already have materials and resources to help get started. For example, how about organizing a holiday food drive for a local food bank or homeless shelter? Lots of groups do things like this around the end-of-the-year, but hungry people need food all year long! Your

<=====================================[

]==>

organization can also collect wholesome books and magazines for homeless and recovery shelters. Many Ronald McDonald houses collect aluminum can tabs for recycling. They recycle the tabs just like they would the whole can, yet the tabs are pure, high-quality aluminum and they are easier to store and transport. Ask around to see what is needed in your community. It can be disappointing to put in a lot of effort on something that is already being taken care of by someone else.

Here is the point: If you make servant leadership easy and integrate it into your organization's normal course of operations, your staff will naturally find a means to serve in small and meaningful ways. Allow everyone to give into the urge to do something nice for someone else. What could be easier than that? Sometimes leadership is more about getting started than

<==[

]===>
what is actually done. Encourage everyone to get out there, do something and see what paths of leadership open to them. Frankly, this is also a good way to groom potential new leaders within the organization.

Tip Four: There is always time for service.

"It is amazing what I can make time for," said Kelly, "ESPN's SportsCenter is repeated throughout the morning, yet I will leave it running as I sit in a hotel room and watch the same home-runs, slam-dunks, and boo-yah's over and over again. I have seen every episode of Seinfeld at least 20 times, The Blues Brothers and Ocean's 11 movies more than that, and heard Craig Ferguson declare that it is 'a great day for America' hundreds, if not thousands, of times. And I still get sucked in every time that they are on television. I make time for Facebook and Twitter. I make time for lots of

<===[

]===>

things. I also make time to serve others and I have helped lead college students to perform more than two million hours of service."

What about you? Do you have a couple hours in your week that you could give to helping someone in need? Do you have the time to volunteer at an agency that serves people in your community? What skills do you have to bring to servant leadership? There is most likely someone nearby who needs what you can offer. Ask these same questions of your staff.

Tip Five: Be willing to take risks.

"I think the willingness to take risks is an important trait for all leaders," said Kelly, "I do not mean crazy things like jumping out of airplanes, riding Ferris wheels, or battling spiders (OK, those are a few of my phobias), but risks that can take an organization to a

<==[

]===>

new level, achieve a milestone, or just as easily set the group back months or years."

Leaders take chances. Everyone's experiences help shape the type of leader that they will be. Some of those experiences may be considered failures, defeats, or setbacks, but many more could be successes. We all could play it safe, but where is the fun in that? The reality is that if no one ever attempts anything, no one will ever achieve anything.

Conclusion

Do you have the courage to serve? Perhaps this is your moment in time. Just raise your hand and say, "I will do it!" If you have that courage, it has a habit of spreading to others. Sometimes, we just need to know that we are not alone.

<===[

]===>

General Lessons

Sometimes there is just no "perfect place" to categorize important information. Thus, we have this section. The lessons may be general, but the fun is real!

]===>
Compartmentalization

Dictionary.Com defines compartmentalization as a verb that means "to divide into categories or compartments." In business, compartmentalization is a way of life. As administrators, we must compartmentalize everything. Our organizational structure is compartmentalized, but that is a given. Our thought processes also need to be compartmentalized. Done correctly, issues can be handled strictly as a function of themselves and not of any unrelated outside factors.

To better explain compartmentalization in terms of mental reasoning, consider an employee. Any will do. This employee has two unrelated assignments. With the first assignment, the employee does less than top-quality work. The reason does not matter for this example. However, the employee's second assignment

<===[

]==>

is a bit more complicated than they have become used to and asks for help. This is where compartmentalization comes in.

Typically, an administrator would have negative feelings towards the employee as a result of their previous assignment. These negative feelings not only impact the administrator's work, it also impacts the employee's. These feelings need to be compartmentalized. The feelings the administrator had related to another issue should not impact the issue at hand. The easiest way to look at this approach is to consider the assignments as entirely separate, no matter the person assigned to them. It may seem a bit cold or callous, but sometimes administrators function better when they disassociate feelings towards any persons when it comes to getting work done.

<==[

]==>

To put this in human terms, here is an example from the author:

"There was a staff member who was assigned two different assignments. I was not happy with the results of the first. In fact, I had issued them a warning because I knew that they had done much better work in the past with similar requirements. As soon as we were finished discussing that assignment, the topic changed to the second assignment and they were handling that one rather nicely. My demeanor switched 180 degrees. I went from disappointment to satisfaction in short order. I later learned that the employee felt that I may have been too harsh. The fact is that I had weighed the results of both assignments as they stood on their own. If I would have taken my feelings of the first assignment's results and placed them on the second, it

<=====================================[

]==>

would have surely tainted the evaluation. Even if the first assignment was satisfactory and the second was a disappointment, without compartmentalization, I could have possibly evaluated a disappointing assignment in the light of the satisfaction of the first."

Not compartmentalizing dissimilar issues can be disastrous in the long-run. The taint from not doing so is usually small at first, but can build up very quickly. Do not allow bad projects to endure in the light of good ones and do not allow good projects to fail in the light of bad ones.

When should compartmentalization be avoided? When there is a stream of negative or positive output. If someone keeps turning in bad work time after time, maybe their status within the organization needs to be changed for the worst. If someone keeps turning in

<==[

]==>

good work time after time, maybe their status within the

organization needs to be changed for the better.

Compartmentalization does not mean wearing blinders.

It is simply a means to avoid corrupting the view of one

thing with another.

]==>
Contract Basics

Contracts can be either verbal or written. Both types of contracts can be held up in court with adequate proof and a trustworthy witness. However, clearly, a written contract is preferred. All any contract needs to be legitimate is an agreed upon exchange. A popular example of a contract is buying milk.

You decide to go to the grocery store to buy some milk. You have in your pocket just enough money to purchase the milk. You take the milk to the cash register. It is at this point that one should consider the aspects of a contract. You want the milk and present the money that you have that equals the cost that the cashier says that the milk is worth. Thus, on the counter we see an assortment of cash and a gallon of milk. If the cashier agrees to take the money and you agree to take the milk, the contract is fulfilled. If either party

<=======================================[

]===>

changes their minds, there is no contract. If the cashier

decides that the milk's price is open to negotiation, then

negotiation must be made to acquire the milk and once a

price is agreed upon, then the contract may be fulfilled.

The receipt from the purchase of the milk is a contract

document that says you paid for the milk.

Contracts need to specify an exchange. If you

offer to cut someone's lawn and ask for no pay, you

have made a promise, not a contract. If you cut the

lawn and then ask for pay afterwards, they do not have

to pay you. If both they and you agreed to cut their

lawn for 20 dollars, they then must pay you after the job

has been completed to fulfill the contract requirements.

The difference between verbal and written contract,

other than the obvious medium, is the legal defensibility.

While not all written contracts are iron-clad, they hold up

<==[

]===>

better in court, especially when a neutral third party,

such as a notary, is involved.

<===[

]==>
Cursing? I Swear!

Political correctness aside, cursing in the workplace is how many people let off steam and sometimes it can even boost solidarity amongst coworkers. According to the results of a CareerBuilder.Com survey aired on CNN, 28 percent of employees curse at colleagues in addition to generally venting while at work. However, 57 percent of those that do curse at work and are overheard by supervisors are less likely to be promoted. In addition, over half of employers believe that cursing makes employees seem less intelligent and reveals a lack of control, maturity and professionalism. (CNN, 2012)

There are a few problems that workplace approved cursing may cause. First, depending upon an employee's particular beliefs, cursing may be seen as harassment. Second, it begins to seep into areas that it should not, including situations when dealing with

<==[

]===>

customers. Finally, it is taken home. Once someone has become comfortable with a certain behavior, they take it everywhere.

Have you ever heard of the saying, "Curse like a sailor?" It is because sailors have been known to speak almost entirely in swears. If sailors dealt with the public, it would make their nation look bad if they swore. It has the same effect for professionals and their organizations.

The author knows this for a fact because his maternal grandfather was a sailor and he brought home the salty language of the sea. He is long dead, but the author's mother has long-since picked up that language. Needless to say, it is embarrassing in public.

<===[

]===>
De-Stressing & Rewarding

The one thing that these serious types of books do not typically cover is your responsibility toward yourself. In jobs where you are responsible for the management of an entity, be it an office, storefront or other people, you need to consider your own stress levels and ways to alleviate them.

Here are a few examples from the author:

"I once worked for a company for three years. It was perhaps the least stressful job that I ever had. The owner and the manager loved me. Sure, I did not get along with one of the other employees, but that employee could not ruin the overall experience of that job. But then the owner had to sell. The new owner immediately did not like me. After three years of doing the same job, the new owner simply did not like the way that I did what I was doing and immediately fired me.

<===[

]==>
As I was leaving and just fuming about how upset that I was, the new owner asked me to come back. He said that it was just a misunderstanding.

I continued to work for the company for another six months and then the new owner called me into his office. He offered me a managerial position. I had gladly accepted it because there was more hours, better benefits, higher pay and I loved my job. What I did not know, or perhaps I just did not see it as a lower-level employee, the new owner was a micromanager. To make things even worse, he would ask me to make changes and then get mad at me when one of his changes did not pan out the way that he had expected.

The stress eventually got so bad that to cope, I started overeating and making purchases that I really could not afford. After eight months as manager, I

<===[

]==>

resigned. I had felt that I was on the border of either having a heart attack or stroke. I would go home and just dread going back into work the next day. It had reached the point to where I was actually having nightmares. Within a month of leaving that job, I had lost half of the weight that I had gained purely by stress eating. In addition, the urge to shop slowly ebbed way and the nightmares had ended. I had finally retained some self-control.

It is easy enough to see why I overate and spent so much money. It was because I felt that I needed to be able to control something since I was not able to control the environment at work. I was given my dream job, just for it to turn into a nightmare. It was such a bad experience that I now discourage people from applying to work for his company.

<==[

]==>

I cannot exaggerate how important it is for any manager to take time to relax and to evaluate their stress. At another previous management position that I had held, I actually had become ill, but I had loved to work so much that I had ignored the symptoms. It was so bad that customers and eventually my employer had to tell me that my behavior was unhealthy.

Upon their request, I went and saw a doctor and the doctor had confirmed the suspicions of the people at my workplace. My doctor told me that I was overexerting myself and that I was just on the border of having either a heart attack or stroke. The doctor told me that I needed to stop overexerting myself and that I needed to take some time off of work. Not just so that they could perform some tests, but to level out my blood pressure, cholesterol and a number of other conditions

<==[

]===>
because while at that job, I was pretty much ignoring my

health.

While I cannot tell anybody else how they should

de-stress, I particularly enjoy video games. Other

people enjoy yoga, exercise, extreme sports or pretty

much anything that they find enjoyable that does not

cause them any undue stress. But another thing that we

must consider is healthy eating. While I may have been

playing video games after work on particularly hectic

days, I was consuming junk food at a record pace. Thus,

healthy stress outlets and food intake is a must."

Once in a while, it is not a bad idea to reward

oneself. Obviously, you must moderate the rewards. It

may be a once-a-month pizza binge, a mini shopping

spree or perhaps a special trip. The goal is to stay

<==[

]===>
healthy in all aspects of your life while not feeling like you are being deprived of anything.

"In the previous job that had been mentioned with the micromanager, they actually denied me of two different vacation requests. They were not long vacation requests. They were just weekends off three months apart. I wanted to attend some special events that were happening across the country. When I was unable to take my third requested time off, I knew that it was time to leave the company. I could not see myself staying with a company that had no respect for me or my need for a break."

If you find that you are working for a company that does that seem to provide you with the perks that you see other people in similar positions at similar companies enjoy, maybe it is time to reevaluate

<===[

]==>

remaining with that company. Because, there is only so

much de-stressing and rewarding that you can do before

you realize that you are not just stressed, you are

unhappy.

<==[

]==>
Disgruntled Much?

All of the mitigation in the world will not guarantee any organization absolute protection from disgruntled individuals. People upset with their jobs or lives seems to occur more often than it used to, or at least that is what we have noticed based upon television dramas and the news. At first it was the dedicated postal worker who flipped out and decided to shoot up the local post office. Then it was the loyal military officer simply tired of what seemed to be an endless war and deciding that it needed to end for him and some of his fellow armed forces members. Finally, we see such acts occurring in the office workplace. In a suit and tie an employee appears and opens fire. The goal of this document is not to place blame, but to respond in a manner that reduces the possible number of casualties.

<==[

]==>
In a general sense, workplace violence is most likely to occur if an organization refuses to take action. The Federal Emergency Management Agency (FEMA) recommends that policies be put into place early on that discourage harassing behavior, insist on the showing of mutual respect and to quickly resolve any complaints. The goal is to foster a friendly work environment by minimizing feelings of hostility, isolation and resentment amongst employees through the use of open and timely communications conducted in a professional manner. (FEMA, 2013)

Allowing problems to arise via delaying or ignoring any issues can potentially lead to a recipe for disaster. FEMA recommends keeping an eye out for early warning signs. These typically include angry outbursts, intimidating behavior, making threats, sabotage and

<==[

```
]============================================>
```

theft. However, for some people, the signs may be very subtle, such as what appears to be depression or simple withdrawal from others around them. These signs may be accompanied by worsening attendance and productivity.

The United States Office of Personnel Management (OPM) recommends that organizations encourage employees to report suspicious or threatening behavior. In addition, the OPM is a proponent for stress management programs in the workplace. Many technological firms in Silicon Valley have made stress reduction an important part of their work schedule. It is a common belief that a stress-free body and mind is also a creative and productive one. (OPM, 2013)

If, in the rarest of cases, all of the preparations were for naught, then a crisis plan needs to be enacted

```
<============================================[
```

]===>
to deal with the worst case scenario. To create a crisis plan, FEMA recommends having planned escape routes, using code words to secretly inform others of a threatening situation, asking staff to periodically check-in, create a resource guide that lists all of the important contact information, having a list of planned responses for each possible situation and to train periodically to remain prepared.

It must be noted that not all violence at the workplace occurs from the people working there. Depending upon how open the work environment happens to be, alternative plans must be made to handle issues with outside parties. This may mean adding video surveillance, identification badges, security officers and metal detectors, amongst other things.

<===[

]==>

In the case of an active shooter, FEMA recommends either safely evacuating or hiding and to only take action if it is the absolute last resort.

Similar to what FEMA recommends, some organizations have created three general actions one must consider when there is a hostile person in the workplace. First, try to get away. Run outside and call law enforcement. If that fails, try to hide and call law enforcement. Be as quiet as you can and barricade any entrances. If all else fails, defend yourself. Turn anything that you can find into a weapon. No one is asking you to be a hero, but your actions may be the difference between life or death.

In any case, remain calm and think ahead.

<====================================[

]==>
Dress for Success

Tradition plays a significant role in how professionals dress in the modern workplace. For example, the necktie was originally created approximately 400 years ago as a stylish scarf for men out in the cold. During the last century a significant number of professional men wore hats and wristwatches religiously. Today, relatively few professionals wear hats unless they work outside and even less wear wristwatches, but they still wear neckties.

The essential purpose of a tradition is to create a sense of comfort and uniformity. Not everyone can appreciate change and even less like change simply for the sake of change. While neckties, hats and wristwatches serve few functional purpose in today's workplace, that have become strictly status symbols. Some research has indicated that wearing a tie, even

<===[

]==>

when applying to a position where a tie would be unrequired dress, is a sign of professionalism. (The Gentle Manual, 2012) Wearing an expensive watch is an indicator of wealth and a nice Fedora hat is a sign of having class. Combining all three items in a formal setting provides an appearance of being a true gentleman.

Women have historically had a harder time blending into the professional workplace. Prior to the 1980s, it was expected that all women wore either dresses or skirts in the workplace. When the corporate glass ceiling was finally broken, it was not unusual for women to dress similarly to men. In our society today, women that can wear a pant suit and directly compete with men are highly respected.

<====================================[

]===>
Gift Exchanges

During the course of the year there are countless birthdays and a number of key holidays where it is sometimes customary to give or exchange gifts. There are both reasons in favor of and against exchanging gifts. The most significant reason against gift giving is based on religious beliefs. There are a few religions that do not celebrate birthdays and certain holidays. To present a gift to someone with such beliefs may make them feel uncomfortable. Of course those in favor of gift giving would also appreciate receiving a gift. To be as inclusive as possible when it comes to holiday gift giving exchanges, be as politically correct as possible and respect the beliefs of those who do not wish to participate in any way.

There are some rules of etiquette that should be followed while planning and then engaging in a gift

<===[

]===>

exchange. First, leave personal items, perfume, clothing and alcohol off the gift list unless specifically requested, such as during a Secret Santa. Second, if there is a set price limit, stay within it. The price limit does not typically include shipping and taxes in its total. Third, avoid religiously-based and joke gifts. Also make sure that what is being purchased is thoughtful, innocuous and functional.

Choose gifts that can be useful in business such as calendars and coasters or gift cards from major chain businesses so the recipient can easily utilize the balance. Finally, if not participating in a Secret Santa, buy extra gifts just in case someone is accidently left out of the exchange and make sure that all of the gifts have been wrapped. Most people find the anticipation via the unwrapping a gift an enjoyable experience.

<==[

]===>

It is best to only participate in exchanges at the workplace that have been approved by a supervisor. Unauthorized exchanges may be seen as a means of shirking work and wasting time, which can mean wasting money and hindering promotion opportunities. Once approved, make sure that someone remembers to give a gift to the supervisor who allowed the gift exchange to occur.

If a supervisor is chosen or chooses to give you a gift, send them a thank you note within three work days of receipt. If you are chosen or decide to give a gift to a supervisor, remember to follow all the aforementioned suggestions to gift giving and also make sure that you have fully evaluated the gift to ensure only a positive impression. These suggestions are also true if a group of subordinates wish to collectively give a gift to a

<===[

]==>
supervisor, but remember to follow the rules of office pools when managing the task of the gift's purchase. Do not give a supervisor any gifts that may suggest that they do not know how to perform their job or makes assumptions about their personal life. Also avoid gifts that may suggest that there is a personal relationship with the supervisor. Of course, if you see a subordinate giving or receiving gifts of a deeply personal nature to or from a supervisor who they are not already in a relationship with, it may be necessary to inform someone in the workplace hierarchy what has been seen.

It does happen on occasion that someone does give a bad gift. Be polite when accepting the gift. Only if in repeated circumstances should you pull the gift giver aside and calmly explain the issue with the gift, such as allergies or religious limitations. If all else fails,

<===[

]==>

ask someone what they would like or tell them what you

would like, within reason. There is no sense in stressing

yourself out. After all, it is the thought that counts.

]==>

Multitasking Is Fallacy

Parallel Processing Is Truth

The human brain cannot multitask. If it could, we would actually be able to focus on two tasks simultaneously and still complete them both with some competency. We are able to switch between two tasks or more, only focusing on one at a time. However, that switching takes a toll on our minds and efficiency over time. Our brains begin to slow down and the frequent switching may cause things to become mixed up.

What the human brain actually allows us to do that could be consider as multitasking is called parallel processing. Parallel processing allows us to subconsciously accomplish a task while we consciously complete another.

<======================================[

]==>

Have you ever tried to think of something and later remember it? Your brain was working in the background. That is a form of parallel processing.

Another form of parallel processing is when you are driving and talking on the telephone or singing with the radio. What happens is that you either sort of go into an autopilot mode or sort of half listen to the telephone call or song. You may not be able to accurately recall your trip, call or song as your brain had moved some functions into your subconscious.

<====================================[

]==>

Office No-No's: A Reference List

You are not going to find an Office Yes-Yes' list in this document. The yes-yes' list of any employee is the one that lists their job description, profile and workplace policies. This list is also not wholly comprehensive, but it is useful for quick reference, most of which covers topics already found in this document. Everything here can impact your position at the workplace.

- Avoid any philosophical debates. Politics and religion are amongst the most heated topics that anyone can discuss. Sports may also be a hot button issue if you do not root for the local team.

- Do not discuss your benefits or pay. Above politics, religions and even sports, discussing what benefits you receive and how much you get paid can infuriate some people, especially if they are a co-worker at the same level as you within the organization.

<==[

]==>

Sometimes pay is negotiated, other times it is based on merit, but no matter how or why you earn what you earn, keep it to yourself. For anyone who negotiates their benefits and pay, informing others about what you earn can impact you via competing offers to replace you. If you are a public employee, your earnings may be publicly displayed.

- Do not touch anyone without permission. An innocent touch can easily be construed as sexual harassment. Start with a handshake to evaluate their personal space.

- Do not dress for failure. Dress similar to the others around you. You do not have to dress exactly the same, but it is always a good idea to dress at the same level, be it casual (street clothes), business casual (Polo & khakis) or professional (suit & tie).

<==[

]===>

- Do not use foul language. Keeping the words that you speak at a family-friendly level is highly unlikely to offend anyone. Some words can be insulting, while others can be easily misconstrued as sexual harassment.

- Do not decorate offensively. Be it a picture on the wall or your computer's screensaver, the family-friendly rule also applies here. Do not place images around your workspace, of anywhere at work for that manner, which may potentially hurt someone's feelings. The consequences are the same as using foul language.

- Do not lose your temper. We all get annoyed with someone or something sometimes. Step away from the issue, take a few deep breaths, maybe even take

<==[

]===>

your mind off the issue and come back in the short order with a calmer demeanor and a new outlook.

- Do not take your work home with you. Unless you are specifically told otherwise, do not leave the workplace with work items. Depending upon the type of organization and its particular policies, taking items that are not yours from the workplace may constitute theft or even accusations of some unethical behavior. Being off work should be about relaxing. Use your time off as it is intended to be used.

- Do not love thy neighbor. Well, for many organizations, loving thy workspace neighbor is a sin. There are policies in some places that discourage fraternization and nepotism. Most organizations find it acceptable in situations where there is no supervisor-subordinate or co-worker conflicts.

<===[

]==>

- Do not get wasted. Well, you can get black out drunk or high if you wanted to on your days off. However, it may be a good idea to be sober for about 24 hours prior to arriving at work. You will never know when a drug test will be issued. Plus, operating heavy machinery while intoxicated is a bad idea to begin with.

- No drama. Most of us have lives away from work. While you may go home and complain to your loved ones about the work day, coming to work and complaining to your co-workers about your loved ones can be deemed disruptive.

- Do not lose track of time. For the exception of maybe Doc Brown, time management is impossible, but task management is not. We are all stuck working within

<==[

]===>

a set amount of time each day and you should plan

out your duties accordingly.

- Do not use your cellular telephone or social media. A

  recent surveys amongst officer workers has shown

  that one-third are using social media at least an hour

  a day. The distraction cuts into productivity and in

  some cases, even safety. So unless your job requires

  it, the safest bet is to log off of social media and turn

  off the cellular telephone while at work. (Yahoo!

  News, 26, Apr. 2013)

- Do not use social media to vent. The exception is

  only if your social media profile is limited to only your

  friends. However, if one of your friends happens to

  be the boss or a co-worker, it may be a good idea to

  keep workplace frustrations from appearing on your

  social media.

<===[

]===>

- Do not treat work equipment like your own. Some organizations provide work equipment, such as vehicles, computers and communications devices to their employees so that they may only have a means of being in contact with work. These items cost the organization money and to treat them badly can reflect upon you. For example, a former local radio personality was provided a vehicle that displayed sponsored advertisements for a local business. The individual took the car out for a drive while he was intoxicated and wrecked the car. The sponsors then pulled their advertisements and the employer had no choice but to fire the individual due to a substantial loss of revenue.

- Do not act a fool. When you are off-site for work, be professional.   You   are   still   representing   the

<===[

]==>

organization in which you work. This is also true if you are off duty, but still wear the uniform. While I am mentioning it, being professional while you are at work is not a bad idea either.

- Do not forget to be accountable. If you are responsible for anything that belongs to your organization, be it property or funds, keep a paper trail. Make sure that someone else knows how you are using what you were given. If at all possible, have a second person with you at all times, especially if it involves money. The last thing anyone needs is to be accused of embezzlement.

<====================================[

Office Pools

When speaking of office pools, we are generally not speaking about going to the company swimming pool found inside the corporate gymnasium.   Office pools typically involve some type of bet being made or gift being purchased as a group of co-workers rather than as individuals.   While the concept of delegating a single individual to handle the cash of others sounds easy, it is not.

We hear on the news from time to time where a group of co-workers have each handed a previously established amount of money to a single individual. The task of that individual was to purchase a specific amount of lottery tickets on behalf of the office.   One of the lottery tickets was a winner, but the catch is that the individual also purchased an additional lottery ticket at

]===>

the same time as the office pool tickets. They now claim

that the ticket that they purchased separate from the

office pool is the winner, thus they do not have to share

the spoils. How does an office avoid this situation?

When delegating an individual to make a purchase

on behalf of a group, they are only to purchase what was

agreed upon. Once that item has been purchased and

returned to the office, that employee may make a

personal purchase of a similar item. It must be made

very clear that the employee did not purchase the

similar item while in possession of the item for the office

pool. In addition, each individual within the group

should receive a copy of the receipt. In the case of a

lottery ticket, each individual should also receive a copy

of the ticket's front and back, clearly displaying the

played number(s) and the serial number.

<==[

]==>

If there is a desire to cover all of the bases and ensure less of a chance for monkey business, another avenue is creating a written contract with very specific guidelines. The guidelines should include the names of each office pool participant, the amount that each paid in to the pool, the division of any winnings, who is being selected to make the purchases and any responsibilities. Everyone should agree, sign and receive a copy of the contract.

Mishandled office pools can destroy morale and create distrust amongst co-workers. Be it a bet or a gift purchase, it is always a good idea to keep everything as fair as possible. It is recommended that anytime money is involved, there should be a second person involved in the process of making the purchase as a means to cut down the chances of cheating. Cheating could include

<=======================================[

]==>
anything from inflating the costs to pocketing the change

to making unapproved purchases. Sure, collusion does

happen, but in most cases having a second person

involved in making the purchase can be a good deterrent

for cheating. It also never hurts to let everyone know in

advanced the costs of a purchase to keep everyone

honest.

<==[

]===>
Personal Space

The space around a person is often considered a safe haven. People often refer to their personal space as bubbles or boundaries, none of which any of us can actually see. One's personal space is highly subjectively and is typically defined by both personal and cultural standards. Young children have little sense of spatial reasoning, but as we grow, we see how others interact in different situations and subconsciously adapt. We know that couples typically invade each other's personal space. If a stranger walks up to someone, the personal space boundary may be larger than if the individuals knew each other. Then there are some people who are much more comfortable than others with how close anyone is to them. However, there are some cases where we cannot read where the boundaries of personal space exist.

<==[

]===>

In a professional setting, standing at arm's length from someone is typically acceptable. It is also true in most public settings, unless in a tightly packed location such as an elevator or subway car. Otherwise, being too close together can be seen as creepy in most public circumstances. It is also encouraged to sit opposite someone that is unfamiliar when at a table. When on an airplane or in a theater, decide who gets which armrests. When space is limited, compromises must be made and it is best to make them civilly.

Most of all, why is personal space important? It is the difference between a harassment complaint being filed or not. The invasion of personal space can be taken as an aggressive action when it is not deemed necessary as part of spatial limitations. Repeat offenses can be penalizing, so if detecting one's personal space is an

<==[

]==>

issue, try walking up to them to shake their hand with your hand extended. Where they typically place their hand is approximately one-half the distance of their personal space. Where you stand when shaking their hand is the other half of the distance. This allows the other individual to define to you their personal space boundary. It is a safe approach that can work for both individuals' level of comfort.

<==[

]===>

Planning By Committee

This topic was suggested by Flea of the Red Hot Chili Peppers. He places group planning into two categories. The first is creative planning. The second is non-creative planning.

Creative planning is meant for artistic endeavors such as drawing, music composition, writing and the like. Essentially, anything where only one can provide the output required to complete. These types of creative works suffer when produced in committee.

Non-creative planning, on the other hand, is meant for non-artistic endeavors such as document reviews, event planning, legal matters and the like. Essentially, anything that may require multiple people to complete. These types of non-creative works are more successful when produced in committee.

<===[

]===>

Red Tape

In some workplaces, getting the simplest tasks completed by those outside of the workspace takes way longer than it should. One would think themselves impatient if not for the fact that others around them in the office and its department felt the same. Some have even tried to obtain autonomy and streamline some processes so those outside of the office would not impede progress as much. After a while, you begin to accept the massive inefficiencies that occur and considered them a result of being a part of a large organization.

As the model of efficiency, one would then simply complete all tasks in a timely manner and submit them to the proper individual at either the office or departmental level and wait. Wait for notifications of receipt, responses to questions and even follow-ups.

<===[

]===>

Doing the job to the best of your abilities, you will eventually stop worrying about the processes ever concluding. Sometimes when you do finally receive the responses that you sought, they were so far departed from their original submission date that there is no longer any recollection of the originally submitted material.

At one point, this book's author waited six months for the approval of an event that was to be held on the employer's grounds. He sent periodic requests for status updates on the approval process for them to only fall on deaf ears. The day before the event was planned to occur, he received an e-mail stating that someone at a higher pay grade needed more time to make a decision. He responded that he submitted the paperwork six months in advance because he needed three months to

<==[

]==>

effectively plan, promote and execute it and felt those three months was plenty of time to make such a decision.

Before he had even submitted the paperwork, he had made sure that the people and space were available. In addition, the paperwork clearly stated the date in which the event was to be held. He concluded in his response that even with permission, he could not effectively plan, promote and execute the event within one day's time. Thus, he had to withdraw his request.

This example was not the first of its type in that organization and it was not the last. However, as has been described, red tape it not strictly an issue of governmental bureaucracies. In a world where an organization lives and dies with the amount of sales and service that it can provide, the inefficiencies of red tape

<==[

]===>
can only lead to one place, where everything goes on sale and everyone is out of work.

If someone submits a requisition form on Monday, on Tuesday the person in purchasing who receives it should process it and get back to the sender by the end of either that day or the next. If the requisition requires a supervisory effort, then an extra day or two is expected. At the same time, someone should be sending the sender some form of communication allowing them to know where in the process the request is as it moves along. If the sender hears nothing by Thursday morning, they need to submit an inquiry and it should probably be in person, if at all reasonably possible. If the process could have been handled entirely in-house, it should have been completed by the end of the work day on Friday.

<===[

]==>

You may have met someone with a background in business management who told you that the best type of business structure is one with a flat hierarchy or one with clearly defined divisions based on broad or major categories. Frankly, they are not wrong, but that really depends on the type of organization that you have and there are some novel bits of documentation out in the world that can help you make that decision. The point is, no matter the business structure, efficiency within that structure is very important. Open communications up and down the chain is essential, but so is processing work in a timely manner.

<==[

]===>
Standing All Day...

Keeps the Employees Away

During the COVID-19 pandemic, a lot of people were out of work. Those people were primarily low paid, non-essential, blue collar workers. They typically held positions where they complete the same repetitive tasks over the course of the day while standing up. This unexpected break in employment allowed many to reevaluate their value as an employee. Many of those people called for better pay and working conditions. In return, a number of organizations met that need by increasing pay by multiples of the national minimum wage.

However, some positions within dollar stores, fast food chains and other smaller organizations still found it difficult to hire to capacity despite raising wages. While pay was an important point, physical pain was another.

<==[

]==>

These stores typically do not offer affordable medical insurance and after any given period of time, standing begins to hurt. Depending on how an employee's body is built, their feet could be the initial source of pain. Over time, that could increase to knee, back and other pains. Some are unwilling to visit a doctor or hospital if they do not have medical insurance.

The research conducted by this book's author over four years concluded with the belief that allowing employees to sit while performing stationary tasks goes a long way to creating happier and healthier employees.

The research occurred inside big box retailers located in north-central Ohio. Over the course of eight hours each day and four days a week, the author had to complete three different primary tasks. Keep in mind that the author did have their legally mandated breaks

]===>
and that is not considered in this research, all things

being equal.

The first task was to "merchandise" products in a

specific isle. Merchandising requires finding, placing and

maintaining merchandise and its cabinetry.

The second task was to stand at attention until a

customer walked up with a question.

The final task was to enable purchasing

transactions. In other words, get the customer to the

cash register so that they can pay for any products that

they chose from the specific isle.

The first and final tasks required a bit of

movement. The second task was stationary and

typically took up 60 percent of the time. That second

task would have been the one where sitting while waiting

for customers would have been ideal.

<===[

]==>

The first year of the research was conducted with the author sitting during the entirety of the second task, only standing when a customer approached. At the end of the day, the author felt no pain from the job.

The second year of the research was conducted with the author sitting during half or less of the time while waiting for customers. The author started experiencing some foot pain, but only after working multiple days in a row. The pain would become more obvious after being off his feet for a few hours.

The third year of the research was conducted with no sitting at all. Not only was foot pain evident while working, typically near shift's end, there was also leg muscle, knee and back pain.

Finally, in the fourth year, an alternate solution was sought. Sometimes sitting was not possible for a

<==[

]==>

particular job. A lot of foot, knee and back pain can be attributed to bad standing habits and posture. Trying different generic, store brand and specialty insoles provided varying results. A well-fitted insole is the solution for most foot, knee and back problems. They can correct how one stands and steps, as well as their posture.

The author once had a job where they stood at least 75 percent of the time during an eight hour shift. Before spending over 400 dollars on a top-notch pair of custom-fitted insoles, they were ready to quit. Yes, it was a large expenditure, but those insoles certainly made that money back by them not feeling so much pain that they were even considering quitting in the first place.

The takeaway was that generally, the more expensive the orthopedic solution, the better the result

<==[

]===>
may be in the short-term. However, a custom fitted

orthopedic solution provides the best long-term results.

This non-scientific research speaks for itself.

]===>

Time Management

Time management does not exist. If it did, time travel would be a reality. We all live on the same plane of existence where seconds tick by steadily minute by minute, day by day, year by year. What does exist is project management, schedule management, task management… I can go on and on. Some may argue that it is a matter of semantics, but in the reality that we currently exist, time is unmanageable and we can only plan for what we hope to accomplish during the time that we have.

With all of the technology available to us, there is little excuse for not keeping up with one's own schedule. After a short period of time, we should understand the issues that make a schedule hard to maintain, such as

<===[

]===>
traffic and other delays. The idea is to plan for most

contingencies when scheduling.

Here are a few examples from the author:

"I know that if I were to drive into Cleveland, Ohio,

I would want to avoid any time between 6 and 9 a.m. as

well as 3 and 6 p.m. during the weekdays. If I must

drive to Cleveland during those times, I know that I

must add 30 minutes to a trip to the west side and an

hour for a trip to the east side. I also know that I must

add 45 minutes if driving to downtown Cleveland. I

must also keep in mind that between 7 a.m. and 7 p.m.,

parking is more difficult to find downtown, so another 15

minutes needs added to find a parking spot and walk.

During major league sports games, I avoid Cleveland

entirely, if possible."

<=======================================[

]===>

The saying, "hope for the best and plan for the worst," fits appropriately here. Scheduling is a lot more than jotting down a meeting date, time and location. Getting there must be considered as well.

When scheduling comes down to new assignment with deadlines, do not be afraid to ask for help or time extensions. Not every assignment issued will be something that you have completed before. Your supervisors need to keep in mind that you are still only human and that the task assigned is unfamiliar. They will either provide you the needed assistance, time extension or assign you a different task. But be warned, do not ask for any assistance until you are sure that you are unable to accomplish the assignment or meet the deadlines. Sometimes you never know what you are

<===[

]==>

capable of until after you have begun working on the task.

If you are still not sure that you can complete the assignment or meet the deadline, ask someone who has worked on a similar assignment previously for assistance or tips.

<==[

]==>

Bibliography

ADA. (2009). *Questions & Answers.* Americans with Disabilities Act. Retrieved on Jul. 15, 2013 from https://archive.ada.gov/q&a_law.htm.

CNN. (2012). *Cursing could cost you that promotion.* Retrieved on Jan. 5, 2013 from http://www.cnn.com/video/#/video/us/2012/07/2 9/pkg-workplace-swearing-caifa.cnn.

Cooper, T. (2006). The responsible administrator: An approach to ethics for the administrative role (5th ed.). San Francisco: Jossey-Bass.

Dessler, Gary. (2001). *Management: Leading People and Organizations in the 21st Century.* (2nd ed.). Upper Saddle River, NJ: Prentice Hall.

Dictionary.Com. (2012). *Multiple definitions*. Retrieved between Jan. 31, 2010 to Dec. 31, 2012 from http://www.dictionary.com/.

<==[

]===>

EEOC.   (2002).   *Enforcement Guidance: Reasonable Accommodation and Undue Hardship Under the Americans with Disabilities Act.*   U.S. Equal Employment Opportunity Commission.   Retrieved on   Jul.   15,   2013   from https://www.eeoc.gov/laws/guidance/enforcement -guidance-reasonable-accommodation-and-undue- hardship-under-ada.

FEMA.   (2013).   *Emergency Management Institute.* Federal   Emergency   Management   Agency. Retrieved   on   Jun.   14,   2013   from https://training.fema.gov/emi.aspx.

Haslage,   Anthony   R.   (2012).   *The 21st Century Workplace: A HR & EEO Guide.*   Lorain, OH: Haslage Net Enterprises.

<===[

]==>

JAN. (2012). *Consultant's Corner: Volume 04, Issue 02.* Job Accommodation Network. Retrieved on Jul. 15, 2013 from https://www.askjan.org/publications/consultants-corner/vol04iss02.cfm.

Kelly, David A. (2013). *The Courage to Serve.* America's Leadership Trainer. https://www.davegonzokelly.com/

Lilly Ledbetter Fair Pay Act of 2009. (2009). *111th Congress S. 181.* Retrieved on Jul. 12, 2012 from https://www.govtrack.us/congress/bills/111/s181#.

OPM. (2013). United State Office of Personnel Management. Retrieved on Jun. 14, 2013 from http://www.opm.gov/.

<=====================================[

]==>

Pew Research Center. (2020) *Dating and Relationships in the Digital Age*. Retrieved on Feb. 18, 2023 from https://www.pewresearch.org/internet/2020/05/08/dating-and-relationships-in-the-digital-age/.

Pew Research Center. (2021) *Mobile Fact Sheet*. Retrieved on Feb. 20, 2023 from https://www.pewresearch.org/internet/fact-sheet/mobile/.

Stone, D. Patton, B. & Heen, S. (1999). *Difficult Conversations: How to Discuss What Matters Most*. New York: Viking Press.

Yahoo! News. (2013, Apr. 26). *Workers Demand Social Media Rights*. Retrieved on Jun. 15, 2013 from http://news.yahoo.com/workers-demand-social-media-rights-101207903.html.

<===[

]===>

Webdings, Wingdings, Wingdings 2 & Wingdings 3

were created by the Microsoft Corporation.

]==>

Recommended Reading

Brunner, Penelope & Melinda Costello. (2003). *When the Wrong Woman Wins: Building Bullies and Perpetuating Patriarch*. Advancing Women in Leadership.

Connell & Savage. (2001). *Does Collegiality Count? Academe - Universities and the Law*.

Cornish, Tony. (1997). *Zero Tolerance: An Employer's Guide to Preventing Sexual Harassment and Healing the Workplace.* Washington, D.C.: BNA Communications Inc.

Dobrich, Wanda, Steven Dranoff & Gerald Maatman. (2002). *The manager's guide to preventing a hostile work environment: How to avoid legal and financial risks by protecting your workplace from harassment based on sex, race, disability, religion and age.* New York: McGraw-Hill.

<==[

EEOC. (2009). *Sexual Harassment & Title VII of the Civil Rights Act of 1964*. U.S. Equal Employment Opportunity Commission. Retrieved on Mar. 20, 2010 from https://www.eeoc.gov/data/sexual-harassment-charges-eeoc-fepas-combined-fy-1997-fy-2011, https://www.eeoc.gov/data/sexual-harassment-chargeseeoc-fepas-combined-fy-1992-fy-1996, https://www.eeoc.gov/data/definitions-terms and https://www.eeoc.gov/statutes/title-vii-civil-rights-act-1964.

FindLaw. (1998). U.S. Supreme Court. *Cases and Codes*. Retrieved on Mar. 20, 2010 from https://caselaw.findlaw.com/us-supreme-court/524/742.html.

]==>

Healthy Workplace Bill. (2012). *20 States since 2003 have introduced the HWB*. Retrieved on Jun. 6, 2012 from https://www.healthyworkplacebill.org/.

Kettl, Donald F. (2005). *The Global Public Management Revolution*. (2nd ed.). Washington D.C.: Brookings Press.

Kingdon, J. W. (2003). *Agendas, Alternatives and Public Policies*. (2nd ed.). New York: Addison-Wessley Educational Publishers, Inc.

Klingner, D. E., Nalbandian, J. & Llorens, J. (2010). *Public Personnel Management: Contexts and Strategies*. (6th ed.). New York: Longman.

Levy, Anne C. & Michele A. Paludi. (2002). *Workplace Sexual Harassment.* (2nd ed.). Upper Saddle River, NJ: Prentice-Hall, Inc.

<==[

]==>

Lies II, Mark A. (Ed.). (2008). *Preventing and Managing Workplace Violence.* Chicago, IL: American Bar Association.

Meier, Kenneth J., Jeffrey L. Brundey & John Bohte. (2009). *Applied Statistics for Public and Nonprofit Administration.* (7th ed.). Belmont, CA: Thomas Higher Education.

Monaco, A.G. (2012). *How to Effectively Investigate Workplace Complaints of Sexual Harassment and Bullying.* CUPA - HR Southern Region Conference: Savannah, GA.

Monaco, A.G., Gaston Reinoso & Becky Hoover. (2009). *HR & EEO Merging to Face the 21st Century.* CUPA - HR Western Region Conference: Westminster, CO.

<==[

]==>

Perry, J. L. (Ed.). (1996). *Handbook of Public Administration.* (2nd ed.). San Francisco: Jossey-Bass.

Philpott, Don & Don Grimme. (2009). *The Workplace Violence Prevention Handbook.* Lanham, MD: Government Institutes/Scarecrow Press, Inc.

Rivera, Zayda. (2008). *Workplace Bullying: Why Women are Affected More*. Diversity Inc.

Shafritz, J. M. & A. C. Hyde. (Eds). (2004). *Classics of Public Administration*. (6th ed.). Belmont, CA: Wadsworth, Cengage Learning.

The Gentle Manual: A Handbook for Gentlemen & Scoundrels. (2012). *When to Wear a Tie.*

Trower, Cathy & Anne Gallagher. (2008). *Why Collegiality Matters*. Harvard University

<===[

]==>

Collaborative on Academic Careers in Higher Education.

USA Today. (2008, Feb. 6). *State action on cyber-bullying*. Retrieved on Jun. 6, 2012 from https://usatoday30.usatoday.com/news/nation/2008-02-06-cyber-bullying-list_N.htm.

Wagner, Ellen J. (1992). *Sexual Harassment: In the Workplace: How to prevent, investigate and resolve problems in your organization.* New York: American Management Association.

Webb, Susan L. (1991). *Step Forward: Sexual Harassment in the Workplace: What you need to know.* New York: MasterMedia Ltd.

<==[

]===>

Back Cover: Why this book?

Since before he even had earned his first associate degree, Anthony Haslage had been helping young organizations, both for and non-profit, prosper. Never one to keep his head down at work, Haslage has gone from organization to organization in an effort of making each organization better than when he had started. Sometimes it took a few weeks and other times it took a few years. While not every one of his supervisors may have appreciated it at the time, a number of them later attributed their success to Haslage upon realizing that the actions that he had taken directly impacted their futures for the positive.

As Haslage worked on his graduate degree, he shifted his focus from helping a single organization at one time to writing articles and books that could help

<===[

]===>

multiple organizations simultaneously. This document is

proof of his change in approach.

If you would like to check out more Internet

Politician content, then please visit our Facebook,

Instagram, Twitter and YouTube social media accounts,

@ARHaslage (http://Tony.Haslage.Net/). Thanks.

<==[